CONTENTS

Chapter One: Animal Experiments

Animal experimentation	1
The benefits of animals in scientific research	3
Animals experiments at 10-year high	4
Introduction to animal experiments	5
Species used in experiments in 2003	5
Scientific procedures on live animals 2003	8
Procedures	8
If mice could talk	9
Animal experiments	10
Animals in medicines	12
Who will stand up for animal experiments?	15
Alternatives	17
The law	18
Concern	18
Distrust among doctors	19

Chapter Two: The Hunting Debate

Hunting FAQs	20
96% say enforcing hunt ban should not be Clarke's priority	21
Hunting with dogs	22
A great day for wildlife	23
Charity angered by deer hunting with helicopters	25
New era dawns for the 'antis'	26
Hunts intend to push new law to the limit	27

Chapter Three: Animal Welfare

Animal rights	28
Animal cruelty law	29
Do your duty	30
Comparison with other bodies taking prosecutions	31
Fashion's new F-word	32
The facts about the fur trade	34
International fur trade today	36
Fur farming	38
Key Facts	40
Additional Resources	41
Index	42
Acknowledgements	44

Introduction

Animal Rights is the one hundred and third volume in the **Issues** series. The aim of this series is to offer up-to-date information about important issues in our world.

Animal Rights looks at animal experiments, the hunting debate and animal welfare.

The information comes from a wide variety of sources and includes:
Government reports and statistics
Newspaper reports and features
Magazine articles and surveys
Website material
Literature from lobby groups
and charitable organisations.

It is hoped that, as you read about the many aspects of the issues explored in this book, you will critically evaluate the information presented. It is important that you decide whether you are being presented with facts or opinions. Does the writer give a biased or an unbiased report? If an opinion is being expressed, do you agree with the writer?

Animal Rights offers a useful starting-point for those who need convenient access to information about the many issues involved. However, it is only a starting-point. At the back of the book is a list of organisations which you may want to contact for further information.

*****

Animal Rights

ISSUES

Volume 103

Editor

Craig Donnellan

Independence

Educational Publishers

First published by Independence
PO Box 295
Cambridge CB1 3XP
England

British Library Cataloguing in Publication Data
Animal Rights – (Issues Series)
I. Donnellan, Craig II. Series
179.3

ISBN 1 86168 317 0

Printed in Great Britain
MWL Print Group Ltd

Typeset by
Claire Boyd

Cover
The illustration on the front cover is by
Don Hatcher.

Animal experimentation

Richard O'Dent explores an emotive issue

Human experimentation on animals is a subject that literally evokes violent reactions: 'I don't think you'd have to kill too many [animal researchers]. I think for five lives, ten lives, 15 human lives, we could save a million, two million, ten million non-human lives ... I am simply saying that [violence] is a morally acceptable tactic and it may be useful in the struggle for animal liberation.'[1] These comments by American surgeon and animal rights campaigner Jerry Vlasak led to him being banned from entering the UK. He uses extreme language, but surveys reveal that many people in the UK are uneasy about or opposed to the testing of new medicines on animals.[2]

The reality is that almost all modern drugs, vaccines, anaesthetics and many surgical techniques have been developed after tests on animals. No new drug is allowed to be tested on humans without animal safety tests, and the development of new drugs relies on an understanding of disease gained by animal research, increasingly making use of genetically engineered animals. What are the facts about animal experimentation, and how can we balance the value of human and animal lives?

Animal experiments in the UK
How many animals?
Currently, about 2.78 million animals are used in research in the UK each year.[3]

The most controversy is about the use of pet species, such as cats and dogs, and primates in experiments. The cats and dogs that make up 0.3% of the total number of animals used each year (8,250 animals per year) are all bred for research; no strays or unwanted pets can be used. Primates (around 4,000 per year) are mostly marmosets and

macaques. Chimpanzees, orang-utans and gorillas have not been used in this country for over 20 years and their use is now banned. However, the use of primates in research is highly emotive: plans to build a primate experimental facility at the University of Cambridge were dropped in the face of protests by animal rights activists. At the other end of the scale, insects (such as fruit flies) and worms are used in very large numbers but this is not regulated at all.

Research areas
About one-third of animals are used in drug development. Animal testing of medicines has been required by law in the US and UK for many years. In both countries, testing became a legal requirement after disasters involving drugs that had not been first tested on animals. In the US an early sulphonamide antibiotic killed 137 people in 1937, whereas UK legislation followed thalidomide, which caused 10,000 babies to be born with severe limb deformities around the world. In both cases animal testing would have revealed these serious side effects.

A further third of experiments are in basic biological and medical research, to discover how normal biology works and what goes wrong in disease. Increasingly genetically engineered mice are used in order to elicit precisely which genes are involved in a process or disease. This information is of great help in designing new drugs. Breeding these and other animals for research accounts for another 30% of the animals used.

The remainder of the animals (5%) are used for non-medical safety testing of substances ranging from industrial chemicals to household products. Until 1998 animals were used for testing cosmetics, but this is now banned. Aside from medical purposes, the Ministry of Defence uses animals in weapons testing, but publishes little information about numbers or species involved.

Regulation of animal experiments
Animal experiments are very tightly controlled in the UK. No one can touch a laboratory animal without a Home Office licence. Every new scientific project is reviewed by a vet, an ethics committee, and finally the Home Office, in a process taking

several months, before any work can begin. All laboratory animals are held in approved facilities that are subject to surprise inspections. Detailed records about the treatment of every single animal have to be reported to the government. Animals are given anaesthetics and painkillers to alleviate distress, and any animal that is too distressed must be painlessly killed immediately to alleviate its suffering. Despite this, tight regulation doesn't make something ethically right. Furthermore, research is a global industry, and experiments that would not be approved in the UK can be performed in countries with lower animal welfare standards.

The majority of experiments are assessed to cause mild or moderate distress to animals; it is very difficult to obtain approval for experiments that cause severe distress to animals, although in some cases animal rights groups have argued that the grading of animal distress has been abused.[4]

The three Rs

The guiding principles used in designing animal experiments are called the three Rs:

- Reduce the number of animals used to a minimum
- Refine experiments to make sure animals suffer as little as possible
- Replace animal experiments with non-animal techniques where possible

1) Reduce

All animal experiments should be carefully thought through so that they answer the question being tackled. Bad experiments waste animal life and lead to no advance in knowledge, meaning that work has to be repeated. Experiments are designed with help from a statistician, so the results can be obtained using as few animals as possible. New techniques, such as bioluminescent imaging and magnetic resonance imaging, can enable a disease process to be followed in the same animal over a period of time, vastly reducing the numbers of animals required to be killed at each stage of the experiment.

2) Refine

Research involving animals has to be designed so that any distress or suffering involved is kept to a minimum, and anaesthetics or painkillers are given after any surgical technique. If an experiment involves animals developing a fatal disease, such as cancer, it can be designed so that the animals are painlessly killed at an early stage of the condition, when they only show mild symptoms, instead of waiting until they have advanced disease. Old-fashioned safety tests, like the LD50 test, that involved finding the dose of a drug or chemical which would kill half the animals being tested, have been replaced by tests in which lower doses are given in a manner that allows safe doses to be predicted.

3) Replace

Much major progress in biological research has not involved animals in the last 20 years. This has meant developing non-animal alternatives, for example in safety testing the effect of chemicals on the skin. However, animals remain the only system in which some biology can be studied. For example, the spread of tumours and safety testing of certain new drugs can only be done in animals. It looks likely that some areas of biomedical research will require animal experiments for many years to come. For example, stem cell therapy requires animal tests to work out whether it can be safely performed in humans.

Are animal experiments ethical?

Even with all these safeguards in place, many people feel either uneasy about or hostile to animal experiments. There are two conflicting contemporary views on animal experiments:

Animals have rights – experimentation is cruel exploitation by humans

The animal liberation movement sees humans as just one of many animal species, with no grounds to claim that we are superior to any other kind of creature. Following this argument, animal experiments are regarded as 'speciesist', discriminating unreasonably on the basis of species. This is considered just as offensive as racism or sexism, amounting to cruel treatment driven by prejudice. Humans should experiment on other humans and not abuse weaker species. More background on this view is found in a recent CMF File.[5]

Animals are owned by humans, so there are no problems with experimentation

The opposing view is that humans own animals, which are intrinsically inferior. Animals have value only because they are useful to humans and, as a result, there are no limits on what humans can do to animals. This view justifies not only animal experimentation, but poor living conditions for a large number of animals in industrial farming, as well as the destruction of ecosystems and entire species by agriculture and industry.

Tough questions

There is no simple answer to the question of whether animal experiments are ethical. Here are two examples of the issues we must consider in building our response to animal experimentation.

Drug development

Can we justify treating humans with new drugs without looking for dangerous side effects in animals? Not to do this places the lives of patients in early clinical trials at increased risk. As discussed above, there have been disasters following failures to carry out appropriate animal tests; these have made animal testing of new drugs a legal requirement. Humans are of more value than animals because of God's own image reflected in us, but animals matter and their suffering should be minimised. Drug safety testing is improving, and the latest mathematical research investigating new ways of modelling drug levels in animals may reduce the number of animals involved in testing. Abandoning the old LD50 test, which required increasing doses to a level where half the animals died, has substantially decreased the suffering of animals involved in tests. There seems no way to avoid using some animals in drug testing at present, but we should support efforts to refine and replace tests wherever possible. It is ironic that chemotherapy drugs developed using animal testing and refined in clinical trials on patients are now used to benefit animals, for example by vets treating dogs with lymphoma.

Basic science

Can we justify animal experimentation in 'curiosity driven' basic scientific research with no direct medical benefits? Many animals are used for such purposes. Some experiments may lead to improved treatments in the future through a better understanding of animal physiology and genetics. However, most experiments of this sort have little relevance to new drugs or treatments.

The degree to which animals suffer is key in assessing this type of work. In 'mild' experiments, animals have treatments that cause no or minimal symptoms and are then killed painlessly. These animals may be significantly better treated than many farm animals. If we allow animals to be farmed to produce meat, we may consider it acceptable to 'farm' laboratory animals for knowledge instead of food.

In other experiments significant animal suffering is inevitable. It seems difficult to justify any experiments causing moderate or severe distress to animals that do not have a very direct benefit to human health. All scientific experiments have to be rigorously designed. Bad science is a needless waste of animal life and should be deplored.

Conclusion

Animal experimentation raises big questions and provides no simple answers. After much consideration, my own personal position can be summarised by saying that some experiments are clearly justified, whilst others are clearly not. This leaves a significant section where I am still not sure.

In grappling with dilemmas such as these we are confronted by the difficulty of the task entrusted to humankind by God, and are driven to ask for divine wisdom in making what are often uncomfortable decisions. To maintain a Christian position in this debate will result in hostile criticism from those with extreme views, both for or against. Nevertheless, I believe this is what we are called to do.

References
1. Laville S. Banned activist defends violence. *Guardian* 2004; 28 August
2. Guardian/ICM Monthly Poll; January 2001. www.icmresearch. co.uk/reviews/2001/guardian-poll-jan-2001.htm
3. www.homeoffice.gov.uk/docs/ animalstats.html
4. Curtis P. MPs urge inquiry into Huntingdon xenotransplantation. *Guardian* 2003; 11 November
5. Misselbrook D. *Speciesism*. CMF Files 26. London: CMF, 2004

■ Dr Richard O'Dent is a UK-based medical researcher

■ The above information is from *Nucleus*, October 2004, pp20-26 by the Christian Medical Fellowship. For further information visit their website: www.cmf.org.uk

The benefits of animals in scientific research

There is considerable concern about the use of animals in scientific research, and all too often it is easy to lose sight of the advantages that have been generated through this work with animals.

Behind the scare stories and myths there lies an ever growing number of successes and advances in the field of human medicine. For many years, humans have been benefited from the healthcare advances that animal-based research has achieved.

For example, here is a list of the average number of operations performed in the UK in a year:

■ 3,000,000 operations under general anaesthetic
■ 90,000 cataract operations
■ 60,000 joint replacements
■ 13,000 coronary bypasses
■ 10,000 pacemakers implanted
■ 6,000 heart valve repairs or replacements
■ 4,000 heart defects corrected
■ 2,500 corneal transplants
■ 2,000 kidney transplants
■ 400 heart/lung transplants

None of these operations or the techniques used during them would have been possible without previous animal research. It is likely that many of us will come into contact with someone who has benefited from these advances. The contribution that animals have made to human wellbeing is immense.

Advances continue to be made. Key-hole surgery, organ transplantation, skin grafting and the latest research into the prevention of genetic diseases are all benefiting from animal research.

It is certain that any unnecessary reduction in the amount of research would have serious consequences for future research into human illness and wellbeing.

■ The above information is from Huntingdon Life Sciences' website which can be found at www.huntingdon.com

Animal experiments at 10-year high

The number of animal experiments in the UK has risen to its highest level for 10 years, figures showed on 8 September 2004.

The total in 2003 rose by 59,000 to 2.79 million, an increase of 2.2 per cent on 2002, the Home Office data showed.

The number of experiments involving monkeys and other primates rose by almost 20 per cent to 4,799, although the numbers used for the first time in experiments fell by 100.

The figures were defended by scientists but condemned by animal rights' groups including the RSPCA, which said they were 'unacceptable'.

The vast majority of the experiments, 85 per cent, involved mice, rats and other rodents.

About 70 per cent of the primates are used by the drug industry.

The Government's Animal Procedures Committee recommends that primate research be phased out eventually.

Caroline Flint, the Home Office minister, said: 'There remains a clear need for the use of animals in vital scientific research where no alternative is available. This type of research saves countless lives each year.'

'It must be everybody's objective that the numbers of animals used in research should in the long run fall,' said Prof Colin Blakemore, chief executive of the Medical Research Council. 'Everyone hopes that a time will come when no animal is used at all.'

However, he told the British Association's annual meeting in Exeter that a rise in the number of procedures was expected because GM animals, mostly rodents, were becoming indispensable in understanding basic genetic mechanisms and the quest to cure cancer, Alzheimer's disease, cystic fibrosis and other illnesses.

By Roger Highfield and David Derbyshire

GM animals were used in 764,000 procedures, representing 27 per cent of all procedures for 2003, compared with eight per cent in 1995.

Anti-vivisectionists said the statistics did not paint an honest picture of animal suffering, a view shared by Prof Michael Banner, the chairman of the Animal Procedures Committee, which advises the Government on animal research.

> **The vast majority of the experiments, 85 per cent, involved mice, rats and other rodents. About 70 per cent of the primates are used by the drug industry**

In *The Daily Telegraph* in September 2004, Prof Banner wrote: 'Official statistics do not answer the two questions central to this debate: to what extent do animals suffer in the experiments? And how many animals are subjected to experiments that make them suffer?'

However, he agreed that the bald figure that there were 2,790,000 procedures conjured up an image of suffering on a vast scale when the term procedure included taking a blood sample, altering diet and breeding animals.

The British Union for the Abolition of Vivisection criticised the Government for its 'utter failure to tackle the issue of animal experiments. The lab animal death toll continues to go up and up.'

Penny Hawkins of the RSPCA said: 'The most disturbing figure is the 20 per cent increase in procedures using primates – this is the most procedures carried out on primates since the mid-1990s. An increase in experiments on primates should not be acceptable in a humane society.'

Dan Lyons, the director of Uncaged Campaigns, the group against vivisection, said that animal research was 'completely out of control' in Britain. Claims of 'strict regulation' by the Government were 'cynical lies designed to fool the public into thinking that animal experiments are a medical necessity and that suffering is minimal'.

Introduction to animal experiments

Information from the British Union for the Abolition of Vivisection

In 2003 almost 2.8 million experimental procedures were carried out on living animals in Great Britain. This number has increased by 166,000 procedures since 2001 and is the highest number of experiments recorded since 1994. Over 60% of these procedures were undertaken without the animal being given any anaesthetic.[1] These experiments were performed in three main areas of research: to try to increase scientific knowledge, to develop new products and to test the safety of new products and their ingredients.

Because of the pain and suffering involved in such experiments, legislation requires each procedure to be licensed. For example, animals may be electrocuted, deprived of food and water, surgically mutilated, exposed to radiation, burned and scalded, deliberately wounded, exposed to nerve gas, infected with deadly diseases and poisoned with products as varied as household cleaners, weed killers and drugs.

What kinds of animals are used?

All kinds of animals are used, including dogs, cats, horses, monkeys, donkeys, pigs, sheep, hamsters, mice, rats and frogs. The numbers in the table are for some of the species used in just one year in Britain. In Europe it is estimated that the number is 10 million and world-wide, it is estimated that over a hundred million animals are used in experiments every year.

Where do they come from?

i. Breeding in the laboratory

Many animals are bred directly in the facilities that are using them. Breeding animals and their young may even be kept in cages in the same rooms as those animals enduring experimental procedures. The animals may be born, live and die or

be killed within the same facility or even room in the laboratory.

ii. Commercial breeding

Many other animals are purpose bred and supplied by specialist companies almost on a made-to-order basis with the animals sold as 'products'. They may have to endure long and stressful journeys to reach the laboratory. Economic considerations are a major

---

All kinds of animals are used, including dogs, cats, horses, monkeys, donkeys, pigs, sheep, hamsters, mice, rats and frogs

---

factor in the use of laboratory animals. A laboratory mouse costs approximately £1.40, a cat about £100 and a beagle dog around £800. Animals are bred for particular qualities relevant to research needs. For example, rabbits are relatively cheap and docile and their large eyes, which cannot produce tears, makes them popular for irritancy tests, as they are unable to wash away, naturally, any product dripped into the eye.[2]

iii. Non-purpose-bred animals

There has been a history of concern about pet stealing as a source of supply for laboratories. Certainly there have been many examples of non-purpose-bred animals being used in experiments. In 1989 the BUAV obtained proof that ex-racing greyhounds were being sent for vivisection after they retired from the track.[3] From 1990 all laboratories have been required to buy their cats and dogs from breeding establishments and suppliers licensed by the Home Office. However, exceptions can be and are granted.

Species used in experiments in 2003

Species used	Total number of animals in 2003
Dogs	5,088
Rabbits	17,010
Guinea Pigs	32,894
Birds	120,254
Primates	3,073
Rats	486,362
Mice	1,809,795
Ferrets	1,085
Cats	547
Fish	173,550
Horses	405

Source: BUAV

(iv) Wild animals

Some animals are trapped in the wild, particularly primates. The methods used are cruel and indiscriminate and a threat to some endangered species. Once captured many animals that are considered unsuitable for research are killed needlessly. Others die from disease, stress and inadequate care during transport. The BUAV has estimated that up to 80% of primates caught in the wild may die before reaching the laboratory.

Where do they go?

All premises conducting animal experiments have to hold a licence granted by the Home Office. The following percentages are from the total number of procedures started in 2003. They were carried out by:

i   Commercial companies (36%) – who run contract testing laboratories involved in testing new products such as drugs, agrochemicals and household products.

ii Universities (40.5%) – who have their own laboratories for educational and research purposes. They are also commissioned to do research by external bodies such as commercial companies and medical charities.

iii Government departments (2.6%) – this figure includes work done in Public Health laboratories and NHS hospitals. Government departments have their own laboratories and research centres, for example, the Department for Environment, Food & Rural Affairs (DEFRA) has laboratories for research such as developing new breeds of farm animals and for testing new agricultural chemicals.

iv Charities (5%) – may have their own laboratories and also commission research projects in universities (this university research is included under the Universities figure and not in the above figure).

v   Other public bodies (14.6%)

Do animal experiments work?

Experiments on animals are unreliable because they tell us about animals, not people. For example, aspirin causes birth defects in rats and mice, but not in humans, while penicillin, which is a life saver in humans, is poisonous to guinea pigs.

> *Animals are usually selected on the grounds of convenience and cost, the vast majority of animals used being mice and rats, and not on the basis of their 'human similarities'*

A senior executive of a leading drug company GlaxoSmithKline recently admitted that more than 90% of drugs only work in 30-50% of people.[4] These drugs would have been passed as 'safe' and 'effective' by animal tests.

Some tests are designed in such a way that the results are clearly dubious, long before the test is carried out, such as when animals in toxicity testing are force-fed unrealistically high volumes of a substance. For example, in one poisoning test, rats were dosed with over 5,900 times the human consumption rate of hydrogen peroxide to test teeth whitener. The rats experienced breathing difficulties, inability to turn over when placed on their backs, partial eye closure, blood in their urine, and incontinence. Three of the 22 animals died within 48 hours from gastric haemorrhaging.[5]

Animals are usually selected on the grounds of convenience and cost, the vast majority of animals used being mice and rats, and not on the basis of their 'human similarities'. The results produced by animal experiments are both crude and unreliable. They provide no guarantee that a product will be safe or effective for humans.

Are animal experiments cruel?

Animal experiments have to be licensed under the Animals (Scientific Procedures) Act 1986 and they are referred to as 'regulated procedures' and by definition may cause an animal 'pain, suffering, distress or lasting harm'.[6] Over 60% of all procedures are regularly carried out without any anaesthetic. In

Cosmetics, Toiletries

reality the legislation is there to protect the researchers because it allows them to inflict pain and suffering on animals that would be considered cruel and prosecutionable outside the laboratory walls. The animals involved will either die as a result of the experiment or be deliberately killed afterwards, often for post-mortem examination

As well as enduring painful experiments, animals can also suffer from their everyday existence in the unnatural conditions and surroundings of the laboratory where there may often be no natural light, confined space and limited social and/or environmental stimuli. All of these things cause the animals stress, they too can experience fear, boredom, depression and psychological stress and the totality of suffering can be immeasurable . . .

Are they morally justifiable?

Although other animals differ from humans in important ways, there are also similarities. They can clearly feel physical pain and, in varying capacities, also experience fear, stress, pleasure and affection. It is with this knowledge and indeed because of it, that scientists perform animal experiments.

Is it morally justifiable to inflict such suffering on another living creature? Scientists would argue that it is, because of the potential benefits to human beings. But, if this is so, why should we not also experiment on human beings, who will yield much more relevant results? That we do not extend our morality to other species can only be explained in terms of simple prejudice. There is no other rational explanation.

Ultimately, say the scientists, it is a choice between a human and a mouse. Whose survival is more important? Vivisection never delivers the straight choice between a human and a mouse. Instead it is about deliberately inflicting suffering and ultimately death on thousands if not millions of all kinds of different species of animals with no more than the mere hope that that immense collective suffering may in some way lead to a greater understanding of a given human disease. The real choice

Ultimately, say the scientists, it is a choice between a human and a mouse. Whose survival is more important?

is between good science and bad science. Whether to continue to fund cruel and unreliable animal tests on millions of animals every year or to use and develop instead more humane and reliable non-animal methods of direct relevance to people.

What are the alternatives?

Firstly, we must consider whether the test is really necessary. Many experiments are performed merely to satisfy academic curiosity, to fulfil a bureaucratic demand or because results of similar tests have been kept secret. A huge number relate to the production of products which are just minor variations of those already available (i.e. *me-too* drugs). Non-animal research techniques are also overlooked because a company may claim that they are inconvenient or more expensive compared to animal tests.

A wide variety of useful research techniques, which do not use animals, already exists and has further potential for development, if funding were to be diverted to cell and tissue cultures, test tube techniques and sophisticated computer models. Clinical studies involving human patients are also very important. People who are ill can be observed very closely, to locate the cause and possible treatment. New drugs developed using test tube techniques

can also be administered in small quantities to observe the effects. This is already what happens after animal tests and it is the most crucial stage of research.

Perhaps most importantly of all, much more could be done to prevent illness and disease. Studies of human populations can reveal the causes of ill health. This was how it was established that smoking causes lung cancer. Cancer and heart disease are the major killers in Britain, yet there is considerable evidence to show that they are largely preventable. Greater emphasis on prevention could save many thousands of lives each year.

Conclusion

Animal experiments are widely used in Britain and many other countries. As a result, millions of animals suffer great pain, misery and death. The morality of such experiments must be questioned. So too must the relevance and the reliability of the results. More resources must be directed towards epidemiological (population) studies and using and developing non-animal methods of research.

References

1 Home Office, *Statistics of Scientific Procedures on Living Animals Great Britain*, 2003. The Stationery Office.
2 Sharpe R, (1988), *The Cruel Deception*, Thorsons Publishing Group.
3 Liberator (1989) BUAV
4 http://news.bbc.co.uk/2/hi/health/3299945.stm
5 DV Cherry et al. (1993) Acute toxicological effects of ingested tooth whiteners in female rats. *J Dent Res* 72:1298-1303.
6 Animal (Scientific Procedures) Act 1986, Her Majesty's Stationery Office, London.

■ More detailed information on many of the different issues relating to animal experimentation which are touched on here can be found in BUAV's other fact sheets. For more information visit their website at www.buav.org, alternatively, contact them at the address shown on page 41.

© BUAV

Scientific procedures on live animals 2003

Main points

- The number of scientific procedures started in 2003 was just over 2.79 million, a rise of about 59,000 (2.2 per cent) on 2002. Although there has been a significant reduction in the annual number of experiments or scientific procedures since 1976, this trend has levelled out in recent years, and currently numbers fluctuate year by year.
- Mice, rats and other rodents were used in the majority of procedures – 85 per cent of the total. Most of the remaining procedures used fish (6 per cent), and birds (4 per cent).
- Dogs, cats, horses and non-human primates, afforded special protection by the Act, were collectively used in less than 1 per cent of the procedures. The number of such animals used for the first time decreased from 9,900 in 2002 to 9,100 – an 8 per cent decrease; and since 1995 there has been a 27 per cent decrease in such use.
- The number of procedures using non-human primates was 4,799, up 822 from 2002; with pharmaceutical research, development and safety evaluation accounting for 3,428 (71 per cent) of these procedures. Since 1995 there has been a 24 per cent fall in the numbers of primates used for the first time.
- Over 99 per cent of procedures carried out on animals listed in Schedule 2 of the Act used animals acquired from designated sources in the United Kingdom.
- Genetically normal animals were used in 1,749,000 regulated procedures representing 63 per cent of all procedures for 2003 (compared with 65 per cent in 2002 and 84 per cent in 1995).
- Species with harmful, but naturally-occurring, genetic mutations were used in 279,000 regulated procedures, representing 10 per cent of all procedures for 2003. Rodents were used in 92 per cent of the procedures using animals with harmful genetic mutations.
- Genetically modified animals were used in 764,000 regulated procedures representing 27 per cent of all procedures for 2003 (compared with 26 per cent in 2002 and 8 per cent in 1995). Rodents were used in 98 per cent of the procedures using animals which were genetically modified.
- Just under one-third (32 per cent) of the genetically modified animals were used in scientific procedures other than the maintenance of breeding colonies.
- About 41 per cent of all procedures used some form of anaesthesia to alleviate the severity of the interventions. For many of the remaining procedures the use of anaesthesia would have increased the animal welfare cost of the procedure.
- Non-toxicological procedures accounted for about 84 per cent of the procedures carried out in 2003, with the main areas of use being for immunological studies, pharmaceutical research and development, and cancer research. This contrasts with 75 per cent of procedures being for a nontoxicological purpose in 1995.
- Procedures for toxicological purposes accounted for 16 per cent of all procedures started in 2003; this contrasts with 25 per cent of procedures being for a non-toxicological purpose in 1995.
- About 63 per cent of toxicological procedures were for pharmacological safety and efficacy evaluation in 2003.
- Five out of every six toxicological procedures were performed to conform to legal or regulatory requirements.

© Crown copyright

> **The number of scientific procedures started in 2003 was just over 2.79 million, a rise of about 59,000 on 2002**

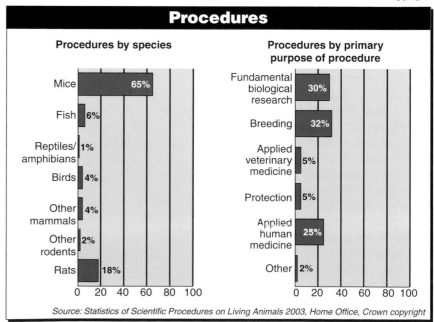

Procedures

Procedures by species

- Mice 65%
- Fish 6%
- Reptiles/amphibians 1%
- Birds 4%
- Other mammals 4%
- Other rodents 2%
- Rats 18%

Procedures by primary purpose of procedure

- Fundamental biological research 30%
- Breeding 32%
- Applied veterinary medicine 5%
- Protection 5%
- Applied human medicine 25%
- Other 2%

Source: Statistics of Scientific Procedures on Living Animals 2003, Home Office, Crown copyright

If mice could talk

If protests force vivisectionists out of Britain, it would be to the great detriment of humans and animals alike. By Heather Tomlinson

I don't fit easily into the animal rights lobby's stereotype of a sadistic pro-vivisectionist: I don't eat meat, and when I was studying for a molecular biology degree I opted out of animal experiments knowing my future career would not be spent in medical research so I couldn't justify my participation.

And as someone who cares about animal welfare, I am horrified by the way in which violent animal rights protesters are dominating the vivisection debate. If experiments are banned out of the UK, as they hope, it would not only hinder the development of new and effective treatment for human disease, but animal welfare will also suffer.

Singapore and China are growing their pharmaceutical industries and life science academic research apace, actively trying to lure the big western drugs firms into moving research and development – witness news that the Swiss pharma group Novartis is developing facilities in Shanghai.

Any British extremist trying to carry on in the same threatening fashion in China would quickly find that human rights – like animal rights – are not taken nearly as seriously there. The UK's regulations in animal research are among the strictest in the world; the same cannot be said for China and Singapore. Animal rights literature often uses pictures of horrible suffering: monkeys cowering in the back of cages, rabbits with painfully inflamed eyes, dogs looking miserable. Many of these pictures are old or from outside the UK. The Home Office guidelines on how to keep laboratory animals are detailed to the point of pedantry on the temperature, the amount of animal/human contact, the provision of swings for primates, and so on. In my experience, albeit limited, animals in labs are happy to see humans and show no fear.

In the UK, scientists have to justify doing an experiment that causes suffering, and the numbers approved are small. Just over 2% of animal experiments are classified as causing death or severe pain; just over half are classed as 'moderate', where pain would be mediated by anaesthetic; and 39% are classed as mild.

Undercover footage at Huntingdon Life Sciences found abuse by staff and illegal practices, prompting a sustained campaign of violence against the company. Such cruelty to animals is indefensible, but we should keep it in perspective: a proportion of pets also suffer abuse, but the average household isn't subject to the spot-checks or undercover investigations that animal research labs are.

Animal rights lobbyists will say there are alternatives to using animals in medical research, but here too their arguments are flawed. They point to computer programs that mimic the human body, cultures of human tissue in Petri dishes, and human bodily receptors that can be put in test tubes to see what the drug would do. All these methods are now available, but we are a long way from the point where they can replace animals entirely.

Animals and humans are different, the anti-vivisectionists say, and it is true that a result in an animal does not mean the human will respond in the same way. However, the activists pick examples from the millions of experiments that have been done that argue their point, but rarely look comprehensively at the data.

A published analysis by the Medical Research Council and industry scientists found that on average animals can predict 70% of the side effects in humans. As scientific progress continues, one hopes that animal experiments will be gradually replaced. Anti-vivisectionists would do better supporting the more thoughtful animal rights groups, like the Dr Hadwen Trust, which raise money to try to accelerate this change.

Pharmaceuticals companies are profit-driven; they don't like wasting money. Keeping animals and doing the experiments are expensive, so they would only use them when there is a clear objective – either finding new drugs, or when they are required by law. The animal rights lobby argues that new drugs usually just mimic existing ones; there is some truth in this, but it is nonsense to imply that all new drugs on the market are similar to existing ones.

Ask the rheumatoid arthritis patients on Remicade, who have been released from a life of pain, or the cancer patients who took Glivec, literally life-saving for those with a certain type of leukemia. One 'scientific' animal rights activist told me that Glivec was developed without the use of animals, and showed that vivisection is unnecessary. This betrayed a total lack of understanding of how the drug was developed. First, scientists had to understand the disease, and animal experiments were vital in this process. The choice is clear: no dead mice and no Glivec; no dead mice in the UK, but more animal suffering overseas and Glivec; or well-regulated vivisection in British labs and Glivec. You decide.

■ Heather Tomlinson is a *Guardian* business reporter specialising in the pharmaceutical industry

© Guardian Newspapers Limited 2005

Animal experiments

Frequently asked questions

Some of the most common questions relating to animal experiments are answered below:

Q. Surely it is all right to experiment on animals? After all people are more important than animals

A. Each life is precious to the one who is living it – whether animal or human. And because animals have the capacity to suffer, it is wrong to inflict pain on them. Your brother or sister may be more important to you than someone you don't know, but that doesn't make it morally right to experiment on a complete stranger!

Q. So you're saying we should experiment on people?

A. No. It is not necessary to undertake tests on animals or people in the early stages of drug development There are a whole range of alternatives available, including the use of human tissue, which are more reliable than using animals. Of course, the final test before new medicines are approved are clinical trials in people.

Q. Would you rather let your child die than experiment on an animal?

A. Such artificial moral dilemmas are often quoted to emotionally

blackmail people into accepting animal experiments. In fact, with the constant risk of misleading predictions, the real choice is not between dogs and babies, but between good and bad science. Vivisection is bad science because it only tells us about animals and not about people.

Q. Aren't animals essential for drug safety tests because test tube alternatives cannot mimic effects on the whole body?

A. It is true animal tests give results about the whole body, but it is the

---

Each life is precious to the one who is living it – whether animal or human

---

wrong body, and human beings are likely to respond quite differently.

Living organisms are complex systems, which is why unpredictable differences occur between species. Scientists can, however, try to make in-vitro (test tube) systems more closely resemble a living person. Sometimes chemicals only become hazardous when they are broken down or metabolised by the liver, so researchers include liver cells in their in-vitro tests to mimic the body's metabolic processes.

Our bodies are made up of billions of cells. Cells and tissue can be painlessly removed from different organs in the body during surgery, biopsies or postmortems. Grown outside the body in the test tube in a special fluid containing all the substances required for the cells to survive, cell and tissue preservation technology is now so advanced that many different types of cells can be kept alive almost indefinitely. By culturing complex mixtures and layers of cells, scientists can create very realistic models of parts of the human body which can be used for research and testing purposes. A good example is cancer research. The use of human cancer cells is proving much more reliable than animal studies.

Toxicity tests for drugs can be done using living cells from the human organs most likely to be affected, such as the liver, kidneys, skin and blood.

Human tissue is now used to produce vaccines and antibodies, and scientists are working with human tissue to replace damaged and worn-out hip and knee joints, and to replace skin in burns treatment and research.

Ultimately, whatever pre-liminary tests are carried out, the first really valid assessment comes when the drug is given to human volunteers and patients during clinical trials.

Q. Isn't it true that there are many similarities between us and other animals?
A. Yes indeed. We all have hearts and lungs and kidneys and blood etc. but differences at the cellular and molecular level can affect the chemical reaction of medications and this is one of the reasons why results from animals can never be reliably transferred to people.

Q. What about experimenting on animals to help other animals?
A. It is wrong to make healthy animals sick in an attempt to help other animals, in the same way as it would be wrong to make people sick in an attempt to help other people. Just as in human medicine, new veterinary treatments can be tested by humane methods of research, and then carefully tried out on sick animals who might be expected to benefit. In fact most veterinary research is done to develop products to aid intensive farming, not for the benefit of 'pet' cats and dogs.

Q. Isn't it true that it was through animals we learned about insulin, anaesthetics, transplant surgery, the polio vaccine, cancer treat-ments and other medical developments?
A. An objective reading of history shows that true medical knowledge mainly arose from studies of human patients during life and at autopsy. In fact, animal experiments have misled medicine time and time again

and held back important life-saving information because what was learned from human studies could not be 'proved' in animals.
(Information on medical advances listed above available on request or see www.curedisease.com)

Q. Surely using tactics of intimidation and threats is not the best way to bring an end to animal experiments?
A. The majority of campaigners are not violent and do not approve of such tactics. Of course there are a minority who behave irresponsibly, but there are always extremists on the fringes of every great reforming movement.

Important sections of the media have chosen to concentrate on this more 'newsworthy' minority and so the public's perception is inevitably that 'animal rights campaigners are violent'. Similar myths commonly peddled are that people opposed to animal experiments are 'anti-science' and 'care more about animals than people'. Sadly, media coverage on such a shallow and sensationalist level only serves to hamper a proper debate of the real issues involved.

Q. Aren't there enormous potential benefits from new genetic technologies?
A. The public is being encouraged to see genetic engineering and gene therapy as the answer to all ills but it remains an unpredictable and potentially hazardous technology. While genetic factors play a part in some diseases, the 'big three' killers are heart disease, cancer and strokes, and prevention of these is what we should concentrate on. Environ-mental factors are much more important than genetic factors in

these diseases. Nethertheless genetic research now accounts for a fifth of all animal experiments.

Q. How can you be opposed to experimenting on animals if you eat them?
A. Does the fact that you eat animals mean you can't be against bull-fighting or hunting or badger baiting or other forms of animal abuse? This is a nonsense. People have become conditioned to eating meat from childhood and it takes time to change eating habits. But many are changing to a vegetarian or vegan diet once they know about the cruelty involved in meat production, and understand they can be perfectly healthy without eating animal products. In the meantime, whatever our eating habits, we have the right to oppose animal experiments if we choose to do so.

Q. Isn't it hypocritical of people who say they are opposed to animal testing to take drugs which have been tested on animals?
A. Everyone has a right to the medicines they need when they become ill. This is no less so for people opposed to animal experi-ments.

It isn't the drugs themselves which people opposed to animal experiment object to, it is the process by which they are tested – a process that is both unscientific and in-humane.

Unfortunately it is not possible to live without using some products that have been tested on animals. Even water has been tested on animals at some time, as well as the chemicals that make up the fibres of the carpets you walk on and the additives in the food you eat.

While people can choose to buy cruelty-free cosmetics and household cleaning products that have not been tested on animals, as things stand, when it comes to medicines they have no choice.

■ The above information is from Animal Aid's website which can be found at www.animalaid.org.uk Alternatively, see page 41 for their address details.

© Animal Aid

Animals in medicines

Information from ABPI – the Association of the British Pharmaceutical Industry

Animal research is essential for new medicines

But we recognise that it is not an easy or a simple issue.

Most of us care about animals. Most of us care about people. Most of us appreciate the benefits of modern medicines and look forward to new treatments to extend and improve the quality of life for millions of people. Most of us want to do the best for people *and* animals. This makes animals research a difficult issue.

All new prescription medicines must be studied in animals before they are tested in people. Advances in computer and test tube methods are making a big difference and are always used first. But many of the potential effects of medicines are the result of chains of biological reactions that can still only be investigated in the living body, with all its cells, organs and systems working together. No combination of computer models and work on isolated cells and tissue can, as yet, come close to reproducing the vast complexity of the body.

Most of these more complex effects of medicines in people can be predicted from well-designed animal studies, giving researchers the necessary guidance to decide whether to take a potential new medicine forward to be tested and then used in people. It would be unacceptable in our society – and would not be permitted – to risk causing harm to people in order to avoid using animals.

The pharmaceutical industry supports the use of animals only where the research cannot be done in other ways and then only with care. But if we want new medicines for conditions like multiple sclerosis, Parkinson's disease, epilepsy, asthma, heart disease and AIDS, then animals will continue to be needed.

The need for medicines

Virtually everyone in the developed world has benefited from modern

medicines and vaccines but there is still much more to be done.

Progress in medicines research benefits us all. Thanks to modern medicines, millions of people are alive today who would otherwise be dead. Millions more with medical problems have been enabled to lead active lives. Animal research has played a major part in all of these advances.

What has been done

Medical research has saved the lives of a quarter of a million children between 1 and 14 in the UK during the past 50 years.

Childhood leukaemia, which used to be invariably fatal, can now be cured in 2 out of 3 cases.

Better anaesthetics make modern surgery possible and medicines to counter tissue rejection mean that thousands of people are alive today thanks to organ transplants.

Every year, 10,000 British people are saved from heart attacks by clot-busting medicines.

Diseases which used to kill or cause lasting harm are now rare, thanks to immunisation. These include diphtheria, mumps, polio, tetanus, measles, whooping cough, rubella (German measles) and some types of hepatitis and meningitis.

Antibiotics such as penicillin kill the bacteria which cause numerous diseases. In the past, because of the risk of infection that could not be controlled, even minor injuries caused great concern. 'Childbirth fever', once so deadly and common in new mothers, is now a thing of the past.

Many forms of mental illness can now be greatly relieved with medicines. There are treatments for diabetes, heart and circulatory conditions, skin diseases, ulcers, epilepsy and many other distressing, debilitating or life-threatening diseases.

Even severe pain can now be controlled.

Deadly diseases which only occur in animals such as canine distemper, parvovirus and feline enteritis can be prevented through immunisation.

Over the past decade the life span of people with AIDS has been steadily increasing. In the past few years there have been dramatic developments. Today, with the latest treatments that work against the HIV virus itself, many people who had been very ill have returned to good health and many others are again leading more active lives.

None of this would have been achieved without animal research.

What must be done

Cancer and cardiovascular disease are the two main causes of death in the UK. In fact, cancer takes more than 200 forms and there are many different types of cardiovascular disease. Important advances have been made, but these two areas continue to kill large numbers of people prematurely.

Prevention and treatment of disabling diseases such as multiple sclerosis, muscular dystrophy and rheumatoid arthritis is badly needed.

One person in seven suffers from the painful conditions of rheumatism and arthritis.

One person in 30 has asthma and the rate in children is growing. Despite advances in asthma treatment, around 2,000 people die from it each year in the UK alone.

Malaria and leprosy are just two of the many diseases which kill or disable millions of people.

Advances in genetics research are beginning to give researchers a real understanding of what goes wrong in many diseases that we knew little about in the past. This knowledge is desperately needed so that new medicines can get closer to the root of the problem and therapy can be developed to overcome genetically caused problems.

Continued genetics research is also needed to help doctors decide who is likely to be helped and who will react badly to particular treatments – with potentially huge benefits both for the individual and the NHS.

New diseases such as AIDS and hepatitis C can always emerge.

Development of medicines

The development of all new prescription medicines requires animal testing.

The development of a new medicine is a long, careful process lasting about 12 years.

All new prescription medicines are developed with the help of information from animal studies. It is currently impossible to develop a new prescription medicine without research in animals. To do otherwise would endanger human life and, at the same time, greatly limit medical progress. Mainstream medical and scientific opinion around the world accepts that animal research continues to be necessary.

Our understanding of the body has increased enormously in just a few generations. So it is easy to forget how much of our biology is still a mystery. Work in the past twenty years in molecular biology has revolutionised parts of the research process, allowing a greater portion of the research process to be done using computer and test tube methods. Non-animal methods are used wherever they can provide the required information. Once these methods have been used to the full, there is still more that needs to be known before tests in people can begin.

Mainstream medical and scientific opinion around the world accepts that animal research continues to be necessary

---

Animals are needed to examine those possible effects of medicines that cannot yet be predicted using other methods. These are effects that occur in the whole body – with its many different types of cells chemicals, communications signals, organs and systems all working together – rather than just focusing on direct effects of a medicine on specific cells or tissue.

In the body, a medicine is exposed to a vast array of conditions that we do not fully understand and therefore, despite being technologically advanced, are unable to reproduce outside the living body. Blood pressure, for instance, is controlled and affected by a variety of different body systems, of which our basic biological knowledge is still limited.

Ultimately, all medicines are studied in people, but only once scientists and doctors believe they have a good chance of being effective and they have enough understanding of the compound to conduct human tests safely. Without this information, human tests would be dangerous and unethical and governments would not grant permission for them to be conducted.

Non-animal methods

Non-animal methods are used wherever they can provide the required information.

Many people have heard about research using cell cultures and computers. Some people may therefore assume that, if a pharmaceutical company uses animals, it must not be using those methods. In fact, all research-based pharmaceutical companies use those methods.

Seeing emails go round the world in minutes and broadcasting satellites put in space with ease, it may be tempting to think we ought to be able to put a molecular formula into a computer and come out with a full print-out of what that medicine will do in the human body. Understanding the effects of a medicine in the body may seem a small thing compared to global communications networks. In fact, no other man-made system or natural phenomenon comes anywhere near to the complexity of the body.

Computer research

Of course, we know a lot more than we used to and medical technologies have made a huge contribution to limiting the need for animals in some areas of research. The early part of the pharmaceutical research process, where potentially useful compounds are identified, used to need many animals. This 'discovery' research now needs very few, thanks to developments like high throughput screening, huge robotic screening systems that can check thousands of molecules in a day for any that have a particular characteristic that scientists believe will be helpful in treating a particular disease.

Computers can also design compounds where the necessary molecular structure is known. For instance, researchers may know what shape a molecule must be to block a receptor on a cell, effectively 'locking it' against the unwanted substance that is causing the problem. They can program this structural information into a computer and get many thousands of possibilities very quickly. These can then be screened *in vitro* for other useful or harmful effects.

In vitro (in glass) research

New advances have made it possible to keep tissue alive and in good condition and cells reproducing for a long time in the test tube. Apart from saving animals, these methods are cheaper and much quicker than the animal methods that had to be used in the past. Contrary to what is sometimes suggested, animal research is neither a cheap nor easy option.

In the search for new medicines, non-animal methods are used wherever possible. In fact, modern pharmaceutical industry research, as we know it today, would not be possible without such methods. By the time a potential new medicine goes into the animal testing stage of development, it has already passed through all the available non-animal methods.

Such methods are commonly referred to as alternatives, a word which may suggest that a researcher can choose whether or not to use them. In fact, there's no such choice. The law controlling animal research – known as the Animals (Scientific Procedures) Act 1986 – forbids the use of animals if other validated methods can provide the required information.

These methods provide essential information, but it is not nearly comprehensive enough to make informed decisions about whether, and in what way, to take a new medicine on into the human testing stage. Because of the vast similarities between our biology and the biology of other animals, much of what we

---

Research is a slow, careful, step-by-step process. The methods that are used at each stage depend on the biological questions that need to be addressed

---

cannot learn in test tubes and computer studies can be predicted on the basis of tests in animals.

Research is a slow, careful, step-by-step process. The methods that are used at each stage depend on the biological questions that need to be addressed.

Research in lower organisms

As our knowledge has increased, we have a much better understanding of the mechanisms common to the whole living world. It is increasingly possible to undertake research using lower organisms such as bacteria and yeast, invertebrates and even immature life forms such as chick eggs and frog embryos.

Harmonising regulations

The Departments of Health, along with the pharmaceutical industries, of the USA, European Union and Japan, have been working towards agreement on those tests required by law. Although the different governments basically want the same information, they sometimes disagree on the specific design and the way to conduct a test. This can force companies to do separate tests for

different countries. However, most of these differences have already been resolved, and work continues towards the goal of world-wide harmonisation.

In testing a possible medicine, *in vitro* tests can

- tell whether a new compound has the desired effect on isolated cells or tissues, such as artery muscle or kidney cells
- show certain hazards caused by direct effects on the cells
- suggest the most promising chemical leads to follow

In vitro tests cannot

- tell whether the desired effect will occur in a complete living system
- tell whether the compound will have a harmful effect in a complete living system

Animal tests can

- suggest which compounds are likely to be effective in humans
- give a strong indication of which compounds will not be harmful to humans

Animal tests cannot

- predict with absolute certainty what will happen in humans, nor are they expected to. They allow researchers to get as close as possible to the situation in people before testing an experimental medicine in people.

■ The above information is from ABPI's website which can be found at www.abpi.org.uk

© ABPI – The Association of the British Pharmaceutical Industry

Who will stand up for animal experiments?

We need fewer laws against animal rights activists, and more arguments in defence of vivisection

By Helene Guldberg

Britain's Serious Organised Crime and Police Bill, which went through the remaining stages in the House of Commons in February 2005, will give the police greater powers to clamp down on animal rights extremists. It will soon become a criminal offence to cause 'economic damage', and those found to have the 'intention of threatening or interfering with contracts involving animal research organisations' will face up to five years in jail.

This is the government's response to animal rights activists' campaigns to disrupt the work of large-scale research institutions, including Huntingdon Life Sciences (HLS) and facilities at Oxford and Cambridge universities, whose directors and employees have been harassed. It will also protect individuals from firms that have contracts with such institutions, including construction workers and cleaners. Prime minister Tony Blair says the intimidating tactics of anti-vivisectionists are a barrier to Britain becoming 'a global magnet for science companies'.

The actions of animal rights activists – including targeting individuals and their families by protesting outside their homes and subjecting them to obscene phone calls – are indeed a disgrace, and reflect the degeneracy of their misanthropic outlook.

The aim of the anti-vivisectionists is to stop animal research – research which, so far as human welfare is concerned, is absolutely necessary. Previous generations grew up in an age without antibiotics, organ transplantation, blood transfusion, or effective drugs for high blood pressure, asthma, epilepsy, cancer and much more. These medical advances would not have been won, or would have been introduced at great human cost, had it not been for animal experimentation. And despite what the animal rights activists argue, stopping, or even merely curtailing, animal research will seriously jeopardise future medical advances.

> ### The actions of animal rights activists are indeed a disgrace, and reflect the degeneracy of their misanthropic outlook

Because of the activities of anti-vivisectionists some pharmaceutical companies are asking whether it is appropriate to carry out essential research in the UK. But however detestable and vile they may be, a ragbag of activists are surely not able to hold multimillion-pound pharmaceutical companies, research institutions and the government to ransom?

Call me a cynic, but surely there are other economic factors at play for companies considering whether to invest in the UK or other places, such as south-east Asia? Or is their siege mentality so strong that they feel powerless in the face of a few pathetic misanthropes?

The Association of the British Pharmaceutical Industry (ABPI) reports that during 2004 there were 108 threatening and abusive phone calls and other communications, compared with 38 in 2003 and 23 in 2002. There were 177 instances of damage to company, personal and private property in 2004, compared with 146 in 2003 and 60 in 2002. These incidences are no doubt distressing for the individuals at the receiving end. But considering the number of people who work for organisations that carry out, or have links to, animal research, then the problem is not that considerable.

Also, the ABPI figures show that the number of visits to the homes of company directors and their employees by activists have fallen. Home visits to directors were down from 113 in 2003 to 90 in 2004 and visits to employees' homes fell from 146 in 2003 to 89 in 2004.

It is striking that, whenever the issue of animal rights extremism hits the headlines, it is always the same examples that are referred to: bricks thrown through a cleaner's windows; paint thrown at the cars and homes of research staff; a company director, Brian Cass, being attacked with baseball bats; and, more recently, the desecration of the grave of an 82-year-old woman. But all these activities are currently illegal. In fact Cass' lead attacker was arrested and sentenced to three years in prison. Why, then, would we need to bring in new laws? There are more than enough laws to deal with harassment and intimidation, and if protests involve physical violence then the law is well enough equipped to deal with them.

The UK's system for regulating animal experiments is the tightest in the world. As I have pointed out on *spiked* before, 'Anti-science arguments are given credence and credibility – and a disproportionate influence – precisely because of the defensive climate today, which the government epitomises perfectly.' The response of industry and the research community to the current climate of distrust of medical research is to elevate their victim status – and they seem to have succeeded in winning the sympathy of the government by drawing attention to the intimidation that they face.

After years of prevarication over animal experimentation and a general spinelessness when confronted by controversial issues, the government now seems to want to convince researchers and companies that it is on their side. But the current bill is little more than a symbolic gesture. Of course animal rights activists should be prevented from jeopardising animal research. But introducing new laws is not only unnecessary; it may also allow the activists to gain some sympathy as victims of civil rights abuses.

If the government really is interested in creating 'the best climate for science to flourish' it should stop pointing the finger at the extremists and get its own house in order. For a start, it should lift the regulatory restraints on research carried out in this country. The UK's system for regulating animal experiments is the tightest in the world, and is the main restriction on medical advance. Researchers can only obtain licences if they clearly demonstrate that there are no alternatives to experimenting on animals. They must also show that the potential benefits of using animals outweigh any suffering the animals may experience. Heavy bureaucracy has resulted in scientists having to wait so long to secure approval for small amendments to research licences that research has become outdated, resulting in the abandonment of the research.

If the government really is interested in creating 'the best climate for science to flourish' it should stop pointing the finger at the extremists and get its own house in order

---

Cambridge University also had to ditch plans to build a world-class primate research lab, not because of the activities of animal rights extremists but because of an exaggerated fear of what the activists might do. Following a five-year delay in getting planning permission, costs escalated and the university had to shelve the plans.

The availability of non-human models with similar neuroanatomical and biochemical properties to humans is vital in progressing our understanding of the brain and for developing new medicines to combat neurological disorders such as Parkinson's, Alzheimer's and Huntington's diseases, as well as stroke and epilepsy. But neither the UK government nor the research community has given an unequivocal message of support for such a research lab.

Research on the great apes (chimpanzees, gorillas and orangutans) was banned under the Animals (Scientific Procedures) Act, 1986. The Animals Procedure Committee, which advises the home secretary on matters concerned with the Animals Act, says its goal is of 'minimising, and eventually eliminating primate use and suffering'. Surely its goal should be to minimise human suffering? That, quite frankly, means that the killing and maiming of animals is necessary. We are not talking about wanton assaults on animals, of course, which most of us find abhorrent. But millions of animals have been and will be used in experiments; they will be cut open, pumped full of toxins and carcinogens, and ultimately 'destroyed', in order to further scientific knowledge and save human lives.

There is no point in capitulating to the activists' arguments – as the government and the research community seem to be doing – by highlighting concern for animal welfare. With such equivocation, it is not surprising that Britain is failing to become a global magnet for science companies.

■ The above information is from *Spiked* magazine 14 February 2005. For further information visit their website at www.spiked-online.com
© *spiked 2000-2005*

Alternatives

Frequently asked questions. Information from Dr Hadwen Trust

What are the alternatives to animals experiments?

There's a wide range of general approaches that can be tailored for use as alternatives to different animal experiments. These include cell, tissue and organ culture; the use of micro-organisms such as bacteria; research at the molecular level; studies with post-mortem tissues; computer simulations; population studies (epidemiology); and ethical clinical research with patients and volunteers.

How can you replace the reactions of a whole animal, or measure blood pressure for example, in a test tube?

We don't claim to. Instead, we aim to replace each type of animal experiment with a sequence of alternative techniques and humane approaches.

For example, careful chemical analysis of a new compound, followed by computer modelling of molecular interactions and body systems, plus tests with selected human tissue cultures, can provide much essential information about a potential new drug.

When it comes to the 'whole animal', it's wrong to assume that other animals are the best choice, or that they are necessary to solve every medical problem. Where possible, the careful clinical study of the whole relevant organism – that is, humans – is much more useful and relevant than an animal 'model'.

Why should scientists use alternatives to animals?

Research that does not cause suffering is always ethically preferable. The law in this country recognises that animals are capable of suffering 'pain, distress and lasting harm', and scientists are legally obliged to consider alternatives to animal experiments.

Non-animal techniques are also scientifically preferable. Experiments on other animals do not reliably predict what will happen in humans

because of differences between species, and because the illness is usually artificially induced, so its symptoms and nature often differ from the human condition.

Aren't alternatives merely adjuncts to animal experiments, rather than real replacements?

No. Alternatives have already saved the lives of millions of animals worldwide – experiments on animals have decreased by some 50 per cent in the past few decades, due mainly to the use of alternatives.

Cell cultures have replaced monkeys in polio vaccine production; batches of insulin are now analysed chemically, not in mice; pregnancy tests are conducted in test tubes instead of in rabbits; non-animal methods of producing monoclonal antibodies have saved thousands of mice, and test-tube techniques are replacing chemical burns tests in rabbits, to name but a few.

If alternatives exist that are much better than animal experiments, why aren't they being used more widely?

Alternatives are already being used in laboratories all around the world, and the European Commission has a scientific centre in Italy for the validation of alternative methods. Still, millions of animal experiments continue.

In many cases, appropriate alternatives still need to be developed. But other factors are involved too: an unwillingness to

---

Alternatives have already saved the lives of millions of animals worldwide

---

change from the established research method; a lack of knowledge or experience in alternative techniques; a lack of suitable resources or finances to conduct humane research; and the resistance of those with vested interests in animal research (such as animal suppliers and contract testers).

What needs to be done to encourage the use of alternatives?

- We need high-profile government support for alternatives in the form of databases, training, funding and promotion.
- The Home Office should adopt a more rigorous procedure to ensure the implementation of all alternatives, and to more actively promote and encourage their use.
- A centralised comprehensive computer database of alternative techniques for scientists to consult is needed, along with expert technical assistance on choosing and using alternatives.
- A bigger, focused, co-ordinated, and sustained effort to replace animal experiments is needed from regulatory bodies, funding councils, charities, and scientists.
- Regulatory bodies must be persuaded to accept results from valid alternatives in place of animal tests, and to harmonise their requirements.
- Young scientists and students must be trained in using humane non-animal research techniques.
- The major research councils and charities should provide schemes to fund and encourage innovative non-animal research.
- A comprehensive national system of human tissue banks must be established to ensure an ethical and reliable supply of high quality human tissue for research.

- The above information is from Dr Hadwen Trust's website which can be found at www.drhadwentrust.org.uk

© Dr Hadwen Trust

The law

The law in Britain protects animals from unnecessary use in scientific experiments. Animal experiments are only permitted if the work cannot be done any other way

This requirement is part of the Animals (Scientific Procedures) Act 1986, which came into force on 1 January 1987. This Act implements, and in some ways exceeds, the requirements of the European Directive EU 86/609/EEC. On the other hand, there are laws that require animal experiments to take place, for example the Medicines Act of 1968.

The 1986 Act covers all vertebrate animals – fish, birds, mammals, amphibians and reptiles – and one invertebrate – the octopus. It regulates scientific procedures that are likely to cause pain, suffering, distress or lasting harm. Many of these regulated procedures are the same as those seen every day in surgeries and hospitals, both human and veterinary. Nevertheless, even though taking a blood sample or giving a dose of a new medicine may appear routine, there is always the possibility for an animal to become distressed. Animal technicians work hard to make this as rare an occurrence as possible.

The regulatory system set up under the 1986 Act is run by the Home Office. It covers who can perform animal experiments, where they can do them, and what they can do. Thus, no recently-graduated scientist can work with animals until she or he has been trained for the specific procedures necessary. No company or university can run a laboratory for animal experiments unless it has approved accommodation and veterinary support for the animals. Nor can a research project start until the Home Office accepts the potential benefits justify any distress or suffering that might be caused to the animals.

If it is agreed there are no alternatives, then scientists must use the least number of animals and keep suffering to a minimum (for example by pain relief). Cats, dogs and

Coalition for medical progress

primates can only be used if another species is not suitable. Great apes, such as chimpanzees, are never used in the UK. Under the law, the scientists who have the licences to carry out the experiments have the main responsibility for the welfare of the animals in their care. In addition, every licensed laboratory has to have a senior person (the certificate holder) whose job is to ensure that it complies with the law. Every laboratory must also have a named

> *Under the law, the scientists who have the licences to carry out the experiments have the main responsibility for the welfare of the animals in their care*

veterinary surgeon and a named animal care and welfare officer who are there to look after the welfare of the research animals.

There are laws and regulations in Britain that require animal experiments, as well as control them. For the safety testing of medicines, it was the Medicines Act of 1968 that was the primary legislation. The Medicines Act was brought in after the Thalidomide tragedy. No pre-testing of Thalidomide in pregnant animals meant its horrific side effects were not detected until after it started to be prescribed. The Medicines Act addressed that issue, medicines are now tested in pregnant animals and there has been no repetition.

The Medicines Act has been largely superseded by European legislation and internationally agreed guidelines that are bringing different countries' requirements into line. Details of the European requirements are contained in the Community code relating to medicinal products for human use (Directive 2001/83/EC).

■ The above information is from the Coalition for Medical Progress' website: www.medicalprogress.org
© *Coalition for Medical Progress 2005*

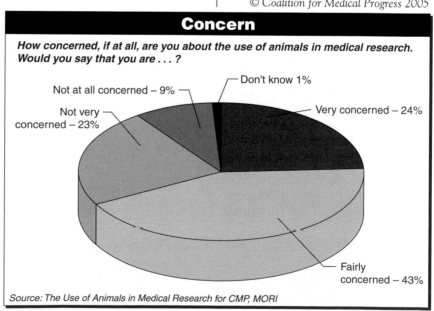

Concern

How concerned, if at all, are you about the use of animals in medical research. Would you say that you are . . . ?

Don't know 1%
Not at all concerned – 9%
Not very concerned – 23%
Very concerned – 24%
Fairly concerned – 43%

Source: The Use of Animals in Medical Research for CMP, MORI

Distrust among doctors

Doctors fear animal experiments endanger patients

A new survey commissioned by the patient advocacy group Europeans for Medical Advancement (EFMA) seems to show that the government has lost touch with the views of health professionals – let alone the public – in its support for the animal experimentation industry.

The EFMA survey showed a staggering level of distrust amongst General Practitioners (GPs) in results obtained from animal experiments:

- 82% were concerned that animal data can be misleading when applied to humans
- Only 21% would have more confidence in animal tests for new drugs than in a battery of human-based safety tests
- 83% would support an independent scientific evaluation of the clinical relevance of animal experimentation

These results confirm that a silent majority of doctors do not believe that animal tests are the safety net that the public and medical profession are frequently assured they are by the government and the pharmaceutical industry.

A recent article in the *British Medical Journal* entitled, 'Where is the evidence that animal research benefits humans?' concluded that animal studies should not be conducted 'until their validity . . . to clinical medicine has been assessed'. This new survey is indicative of this developing scepticism about the value of animal experiments.

A silent majority of doctors do not believe that animal tests are the safety net that the public and medical profession are frequently assured they are

---

Adolfo Sansolini, Chief Executive of the British Union for the Abolition of Vivisection (BUAV), says, 'The early promise of the Labour government has turned into full and blind support for the animal experimentation industry. The BUAV only recently revealed that the government had paid a staggering £85,506 towards a flawed and misleading MORI opinion poll commissioned by a coalition of wealthy pro-vivisection organisations. The BUAV has submitted a formal complaint about this poll to the Market Research Society, as it feels that its leading questions have breached polling industry guidelines. The government is now deaf to the suffering of animals in the laboratory, their cries drowned out by government support for the economic interests of the industry. Dare we hope that they will listen to the professionals who care for the nation's health and lives?'

The Home Office recently admitted in response to a Parliamentary question that, 'The Home Office has not commissioned or evaluated any formal research on the efficacy of animal experiments' and 'The Government has no plans to do so.'

The current system of licensing for animal experiments requires the Home Office to apply a 'cost:benefit' test – under which the likely animal suffering has to be weighed against the anticipated benefit. The BUAV claims that this is impossible without a proper evaluation of the efficacy of experiments and challenges the government to review its decision. Until it does, the government is agreeing to the suffering of millions of animals each year for dubious and 'untested' purposes.

- The above information is from *Ooze Magazine* website which can be found at www.oozemagazine.co.uk

© Ooze Online 2005

Hunting FAQs

Information from the Countryside Alliance

The Countryside Alliance's purpose is to campaign for the countryside, country sports and the rural way of life. Through campaigning, lobbying, publicity and education the Alliance seeks to influence legislation and public policymaking so as to ensure the sustainability of rural life – for the benefit of everyone who believes that a real countryside is worth saving. One of the Alliance's key campaigns at present is trying to get the Hunting Act 2004 repealed: a campaign which harnesses the passions of the rural community, the common sense of the wider public and pro-rural Parliamentarians and the influence of the media.

1. In deer hunting do the hounds actually attack the deer?

No. The hounds are trained and bred to hold the deer 'at bay'. That means the deer stands to face the hounds which stand back and bay from a short distance. This enables a hunt official carrying a gun to locate the deer and to get close enough to shoot it.

2. Why are hounds shot when they are still young? Can't they be rehomed?

Hounds are kept for as long as they are able to be part of the pack. If they do become too slow they are often passed on to other hunts as older hounds are valuable and experienced mentors. Hounds are only put down when they cease to have any quality of life in the same way as any responsible dog owner would expect their dog to be treated. This is certainly not premature for a hunting animal of this size and weight. Opponents of hunting have consistently claimed that hounds would make good pets. The Association of British Dogs' and Cats' Homes who consist of Battersea Dogs' Home, the RSPCA, Scottish SPCA, the NCDL

and others, have a different view. 'The Association considers that the hounds and dogs currently employed with hunts would be almost impossible to rehome and that euthanasia would be an unacceptable alternative.'

3. Does the fox die instantly?

To answer this question it is best to refer to independent evidence. A recent published veterinary opinion on hunting with hounds stated: 'The kill occurs as a swift, almost instantaneous, procedure made possible by the considerable power weight advantage the hound has over the fox.' In the Burns Report, an independent Government Inquiry into hunting with dogs, Lord Burns concluded that: 'insensibility and death will normally follow within a matter of seconds once the fox is caught'.

4. Isn't hunting just a sport for the rich?

Hunting attracts people from every walk of life. Again, the conclusions of the Burns Report show that: 'Broadly speaking, support was highest in all areas amongst men, older people, those who had lived in the area for a long time, people working in rural occupations and those in lower social class bands.'

5. Aren't the majority of people against hunting?

No. Recent public opinion polls show that opposition to hunting has declined in recent years the more it has been understood by the public. Most people believe strongly in individual freedoms and believe that providing hunting is properly regulated or supervised, then it should be allowed to continue. In an opinion poll taken in December 2002 only 36% of those questioned supported the view that 'hunting should not be allowed to continue at all as cruelty is more important to me than civil liberties'.

6. Why can't you go drag hunting instead?

The answer is you can. There are many drag hunts across the UK.

However, the activity is very different from other forms of hunting and should not be considered as an alternative. The Burns Inquiry looked closely at whether drag hunting was an alternative to other forms of hunting and concluded: 'It is unlikely that either drag and bloodhound hunting or drag coursing would of themselves mitigate to any substantial extent any adverse effects on the rural economy or the social life of the countryside arising from a ban on hunting.'

7. Wouldn't the fox/hare/deer control their own numbers if you didn't hunt them?

No. Wild animals generally fare better if they and their habitat are managed sympathetically. Part of this management involves careful control to ensure that the population is neither allowed to expand to such a degree that it can cause damage to other wild species or domestic or agricultural animals competing for the same food source, or to be reduced to such a level that it becomes endangered or ceases to form a useful part in the food chain. Hunting ensures that a balance is maintained at a level that can be tolerated according to regional pressures.

8. Do people get 'blooded' when they go hunting?

No. Although opponents of hunting attempt to claim a ritual element of hunting, there is no evidence that this practice takes place.

9. How can I go hunting/beagling/coursing?

This is easy. Contact any of the associations concerned via the Campaign for Hunting and ask where your local hunt is and then make a direct contact. More and more hunts have now created their own websites. They welcome new people, so never feel that in some way you need to be 'qualified' to try it out.

10. Why do hunting people wear red?

For the some reason that a football referee wears black or a police officer wears their uniform. It enables other members of the hunt and the public to know who is in charge and so that they can be identified over long distances in the countryside.

11. Isn't coursing hares unfair?

Competitive coursing involves judging two greyhounds against each other. The purpose is not to kill the hare and only about 1 out of 8 hares gets caught. They are normally given to the farmer on whose land it takes place to be eaten. In areas where coursing takes place, hare populations are generally higher and healthier due to people's interests in preserving their natural habitat.

12. Is hunting cruel?

All the evidence suggests otherwise (see question 3). The methods of control that would replace hunting (especially in 'inexpert' hands) have been shown to subject animals to a far greater degree of suffering. In his speech to the House of Lords on 13 March 2001, Lord Burns said: 'If hunting were subject to a ban, I have little doubt that at least an equivalent number of foxes, deer and hares would be killed by other means. The number of deaths is not likely to be reduced by banning hunting.'

■ The above information is an extract from *Hunting the Truth*, produced by the Countryside Alliance. For further details, visit their website at www.countryside-alliance.org

© Countryside Alliance

96% say enforcing hunt ban should not be Clarke's priority

A new poll* has found that 96% of the public do not think that Home Secretary Charles Clarke should concentrate on enforcement of the hunting ban.

The poll, commissioned by the Countryside Alliance, asked:

What do you think Home Secretary Charles Clarke's priority for the next year should be?

Asylum/illegal immigration	34%
Tackling anti-social behaviour	33%
The war against drugs	13%
The war against terror	10%
Enforcing the ban on hunting with dogs	4%
Don't know	7%

Simon Hart, Chief Executive of the Countryside Alliance, said: 'The public is clear that the Home Secretary has far more important issues to deal with than enforcing flawed and confused legislation driven through Parliament to satisfy the class warriors on Labour's backbenches.

'The hunting community has clearly stated its intention to hunt within the law until the Hunting Act is overturned either by the courts or by Parliament. It should now be clear to Mr Clarke that the public will have no appetite for malicious or contentious prosecutions during that time'.

Notes: * TNS 21-23 December 2004, 1042 respondents

■ The above information is a press release of 27 December 2004 from the Countryside Alliance. For further details, visit their website at www.countryside-alliance.org

© Countryside Alliance

Hunting with dogs

Information from the League Against Cruel Sports. By Jess Barker, Research Officer

The case against hunting is straightforward: it is morally wrong to pursue and kill an animal, causing it unnecessary suffering, purely for 'sport'. Just as cock fighting, bear baiting and other such 'sports' have been banned, so the equally cruel hunting with dogs has now been consigned to the history books.

Hunting before the ban – arguments

Hunting with dogs is fundamentally cruel. The legal definition of cruelty to animals involves an activity that causes unnecessary suffering. It is clear that hunting with dogs causes suffering in the chased animal, both during the chase and during the kill. The report of the Burns Inquiry, commissioned by the Government to inquire into the practical aspects of hunting with dogs and a potential ban, concluded that the experience of being hunted 'seriously compromised' the welfare of all four quarry species: foxes, hares, mink and deer.[1] Indeed, hounds are bred for stamina, rather than for speed, ensuring a lengthy chase to improve the 'sport' whilst causing the hunted animal to suffer for longer.

The case against a ban depended largely on the idea that hunting was necessary to regulate the populations of the hunted mammals, particularly foxes. However, if control of these species is necessary, there are methods available which cause less suffering. Again, this was the conclusion reached by the Burns Inquiry – that alternative culling methods cause less suffering to the animal.

The extent to which culling is necessary at all is robustly challenged. The Mammal Society commissioned research during the period of foot-and-mouth disease in 2001 when hunting was banned for nearly a full year. If hunting were controlling the population, fox numbers would have been expected to rise sharply in hunted areas during the period of the ban. In fact, there was no significant difference in fox density changes between hunting and non-hunted areas. The study concluded 'These data show that the ban on hunting had no impact on fox numbers in Britain' – i.e. that hunting does not control the fox population.[2]

The legal definition of cruelty to animals involves an activity that causes unnecessary suffering

In addition, undercover investigation by the League Against Cruel Sports has revealed that very many foxhunts provide artificial earths in the area in which they hunt, and even provide food for foxes, encouraging them to breed so as to produce more potential quarries for their 'sport'.[3] Hunting is not about pest control; it is about causing suffering purely for 'sport'.

It is clear that there is no necessity to hunting – there is no reason to hunt other than for enjoyment. It is horrendous that in a modern society the idea of causing suffering simply for human pleasure, for 'sport' should be considered acceptable. If hunters wish to hunt, they can go drag hunting, which gives the enjoyment of riding together with the enjoyment of watching hounds follow a scent. The only difference is the lack of the kill.

The Hunting Act 2004

It is therefore entirely appropriate that Parliament should have made legislation to ban this barbaric activity. After being consistently voted for by a majority in the House of Commons, the Hunting Act 2004 was made law. The Parliament Act enabled the legislation to reach the statute book after it became clear that the House of Lords would never agree to a total ban on hunting with dogs. After a three-month delay in implementation, the cruel 'sport' of hunting with dogs became illegal on 18 February 2005.

The Act makes it an offence to hunt a wild mammal with a dog, unless the hunting is exempt. The exemptions are limited to a small number of circumstances, and include flushing a mammal to guns with two dogs for the purpose of preventing serious damage to agricultural or conservational concerns, using a dog below ground to protect birds for shooting, and the hunting of rats and rabbits, which are not protected by the Act. The Act also prohibits hare coursing – the competitive chasing of a hare by two dogs, which frequently ends with the hare being torn in a tug-of-war – and makes the assistance of hunting by providing land or a dog for the purpose illegal. Those convicted of an offence under the Hunting Act face a level 5 fine of up to £5,000.

References

1 Report of the Committee of Inquiry into Hunting With Dogs in England and Wales, June 2000
2 Baker, P.J., Harris, S and Webbon, C.C. (2002) Effect of British hunting ban on fox numbers *Nature* 419, page 34
3 *Unearthed: Canned Fox Hunting in the Heart of England.* Available at: http://www.league.uk.com/investigations/index.htm

■ For more information visit their website at www.league.uk.com

A great day for wildlife

Information from Animal Aid

The Hunting Act came into force at midnight on 18 February 2005. This is the story of the long campaign that made it happen:

The passing of the Hunting Act in November 2004 represents an historic victory for animal protection. It shows how justice and compassion can eventually succeed, even if it takes a long time for them to do so.

If you sometimes despair over whether barbaric practices like vivisection will ever be outlawed, imagine the situation in the UK eighty odd years ago for those who opposed hunting. The Great War had ended and many survivors longed to re-establish the perceived order and stability of the pre-war years. Hunting formed an important part of traditional life. 'Country sports' enjoyed enormous popularity. In the 1920s, the Waterloo Cup – the annual gathering of hare coursers and their supporters – was one of the best-attended sporting events in the world. In 1927, 8,000 people were reported to have been at the opening meet of the Quorn Hunt in Leicestershire, at which the Prince of Wales rode to hounds.

This was the world in which the League Against Cruel Sports was formed in 1924 (or the League for the Prohibition of Cruel Sports as it was called until 1943). Although there was significant support for the

FACT

Although some members of the hunting community have vowed to break the new law, and carefully monitoring will remain a campaigning priority, the Hunting Act remains a major breakthrough for animal protection.

Society's views – it boasted 2,000 members by 1930 – it had little prospect of legislative progress. It did, however, cause sufficient concern amongst pro-hunt interests for them to form their own organisation to defend their 'sport'. The British Field Sports Society continued from 1930 into the 1990s, when, in a society that had grown increasingly hostile to its agenda, it became the Country-side Alliance – a cynical attempt to present its single-issue obsession as a concern for wider rural interests.

First hopes of success

By the end of the Second World War, attitudes to hunting had altered dramatically. Rather than the longing for an idealised past that followed the 1914-18 conflict, the prevailing mood was for change to a more democratic society. A radical Labour Party government was elected, committed to fighting poverty and privilege. For many MPs, the abolition of hunting was an important part of their opposition to a world based on class. Two backbenchers introduced Private Member's Bills, drawing widespread support from parliamentarians and furious protest from hunting interests. The main defences offered for bloodsports were strikingly similar to the pathetic arguments put forward today. Freedom for the individual to decide whether or not to chase and kill wild animals was demanded. This call was endorsed by *The Times* newspaper. Incredibly, the RSPCA also supported hunting.

Hopes of a ban were squashed when the government withdrew its backing. It was worried that farmers would carry out a threat to withdraw from the national plan to make Britain more self-sufficient in food production if hunting was outlawed. Instead, it set up a committee to investigate the issue. The eight-person team was heavily biased in favour of the status quo and included the vice-president of the British Field Sports Society. The Scott Henderson Report (named after the Chairman) was eventually published in 1951 and

concluded that badger digging 'need not involve any excessive suffering' and that accounts of cruelty during hunting were 'exaggerated'. While it did contain some positive proposals, recommending a ban on the gin trap (abolished in 1958) and snaring of deer (outlawed in 1963), its ignorant and outdated attitudes to wildlife were used disastrously to defend inhumane practices for a further 50 years.

> ## FACT
> Organised opposition to hunting goes back much further than 1924. The puritanical sounding Society for the Suppression of Vice – formed in 1802 – ran the first organised campaign, followed later in the century by the pioneering Humanitarian League. It was the latter who first used the word 'bloodsports' to describe hunting.

Slow progress

As with many areas of social progress, the 1950s saw little advance and the 1960s the beginning of change. The formation of the Hunt Saboteurs (1963) and the new strategy of the League Against Cruel Sports to purchase land in key positions to foil the hunt (begun in 1959) brought fresh impetus to the campaign. But undoubtedly the most important switch of policy by an animal welfare organisation came in 1976, when, after a bitter internal battle, the RSPCA at last announced its opposition to fox hunting.

As animal welfare became a more popular concern, political progress also began to be made. The first in a series of Badgers Acts led to an eventual ban on digging out and baiting, and otter hunting was made illegal in 1978. Hare coursing was almost outlawed as well, when the House of Commons passed a Labour Government Bill in 1975. As with the current Hunting Bill, however, the House of Lords rejected the proposal, one peer declaring that a ban would make the law 'a gibbering lunatic'. Unlike the current Bill, the Upper House had its way when the government dropped its proposal.

Throughout the Thatcher years the campaign against hunting gathered strength, particularly after several high profile undercover investigations in which campaigners infiltrated hunts and demonstrated the barbarity of the practice. Mike Huskisson's courageous exposure of the Quorn hunt – of which the Prince of Wales was a member – proved particularly influential. Video of a fox cub being dug out and thrown to the hounds to be torn apart was shown on national television news, causing public outrage.

An inspirational ban

In 1995, a Private Member's Bill to abolish hunting with dogs passed through the House of Commons for the first time, supported by 30 Conservative MPs. Even though it took a further decade for the Hunting Act to gain Royal Assent, this was effectively the beginning of the end. Backbench MPs voted several times and by a massive majority on each occasion to enforce a ban and were determined to resist opposition, whether it came from the Lords, vested interests or government.

And so, at the end of 2004, the dedicated campaigning of thousands over more than a century was rewarded with the passing of legislation. Even though the considerable influence of hunt supporters means that victory cannot be guaranteed until all potential legal loopholes have been exhausted, the law now stigmatises as criminals those who chase animals and then kill them for fun.

It may have been (and may continue to be) a long, hard struggle, but the passing of the Hunting Act should be an inspiration to all who continue to fight other forms of cruelty. Every ounce of effort is worth it in the end – even though you might not be around to witness every victory!

> ## FACT
> There was even the equivalent of hunt saboteurs in the early 19th century. Strong-smelling pickled herrings (which turn a brownish red colour after salting and smoking) were laid across the likely trail of hounds because the powerful smell masked the scent of the fox. It is from this method of protest that the common phrase 'red herring' – meaning a misleading clue – is thought to have derived.

Much of the information for this article was taken from *Animal Century – a celebration of changing attitudes to animals* by Mark Gold, available from the Animal Aid online shop at a special discount price of £10.50.

■ Animal Aid campaigns peacefully against all animal abuse, and promotes a cruelty-free lifestyle. You can support our work by joining, making a donation, or using our online shop. Contact Animal Aid at The Old Chapel, Bradford Street, Tonbridge, Kent, TN9 1AW, UK, tel +44 (0)1732 364546, fax +44 (0)1732 366533, email info@animalaid.org.uk

■ The above information is from Animal Aid's website which can be found at www.animalaid.org.uk

© Animal Aid

Charity angered by deer hunting with helicopters

The use of helicopters to drive herds of panic-stricken deer towards stalkers armed with rifles was condemned yesterday by a leading animal welfare charity.

The British Deer Society (BDS) expressed outrage that Scottish politicians, who outlawed hunting with hounds on cruelty grounds, appeared to tolerate hunting with helicopters in the Highlands.

The charity has written to Ross Finnie, Scotland's environment minister, claiming that the practice is illegal as anger mounts over allegations that a Scottish Executive agency used flying squads to drive deer towards their death.

Mark Nicolson, the BDS chairman, has attacked the methods used by the Deer Commission for Scotland (DCS) and its claim that it is legal to use aircraft to round up deer towards waiting guns.

The letter refers to the slaughter of 500 deer on the Glenfeshie Estate in the Cairngorms earlier this year. The emergency cull was ordered to protect young trees in the Caledonian forest from the increasing deer population.

However the way in which it was carried out angered wildlife experts, who complained that herds were overrun by helicopters, heavily pregnant hinds were shot and wounded animals were left to suffer.

In October 2004, the controversy escalated when it was disclosed that the BDS has objected to the DCS's view that the Deer (Scotland) Act 1996 allows the use of helicopters to pursue deer.

The row erupted on the eve of a cull of 1,000 deer on the Mar Lodge Estate by the National Trust for Scotland. The National Trust, the owners of the estate in Royal Deeside, has said helicopters will be used for 12 days of the season to fly in stalkers and remove carcasses – but not to drive deer.

By Tom Peterkin

Mr Nicolson was responding to a document sent to ministers by Andrew Raven, the DCS chairman, outlining the agency's position.

> 'No government which has made hunting deer with hounds illegal on grounds of cruelty can sanction hunting deer across country with helicopters as a humane pursuit'

'No government which has made hunting deer with hounds illegal on grounds of cruelty can sanction hunting deer across country with helicopters as a humane pursuit,' Mr Nicolson said.

Hunting with dogs was banned north of the border in 2002 when

the Scottish Parliament backed a member's Bill by Lord Watson of Invergowrie designed to make foxhunting an offence. Mr Nicolson's letter added: 'The speed with which helicopters could drive deer across open country would create an unacceptably high risk of deer being injured, greatly stressed and subjected to unacceptable levels of suffering. As well as believing the use of helicopters to drive deer to be illegal, the British Deer Society also believes the practice to be cruel and unacceptable.'

A Scottish Executive report into the Glenfeshie cull admitted that guidance governing driving deer herds had to be clarified. It found that helicopters were used to 'steady' deer rather than drive them.

But the report published in the summer has failed to placate the cull's critics. The Scottish Gamekeepers' Association, which obtained a video of the cull, claimed the report failed to take into account all the evidence.

The DCS has agreed to draw up a Best Practice Guide covering the role of helicopters in deer management. In the meantime it has agreed to a moratorium preventing them from being used to drive deer – apart from for research purposes while drawing up the guide.

Mr Raven of the DCS said: 'There is really nothing to add to the ministerial report. It is slightly academic because we have said that we are going to have a voluntary moratorium.'

A Scottish Executive spokesman said there was a section in the Deer Act allowing helicopters to move deer during emergency culls, but added that during the moratorium helicopters would only be used in a logistical role.

New era dawns for the 'antis'

The saboteurs

They talked about hunting yesterday with a bloody-mindedness that made it clear they would not allow the ban to keep them from an activity about which they had been passionate virtually all their lives.

They talked about rights, morality, animals and the future of the countryside. They talked about bad law, protests and policing problems.

Except these were not huntsmen talking about their sport. They were saboteurs talking about theirs. At times, they came across as the obverse side of the same coin. Only the accents were different.

And just as the hunts defiantly state that they will not be going away, so the sabs declare that we have not seen the last of them yet – not by a long chalk. Hunting with dogs is down but it may not be out, they fear. Next there is shooting to vanquish. And, for some, fishing.

Yesterday, saboteurs were thin on the ground ('You won't believe it,' said one, 'but most of us are normal people with jobs to hold down during the week') but tomorrow they will be out in force, cans of 'Anti-Mate', if not balaclavas, at the ready.

The essential difference will be that while, yesterday, the protesters were operating on the boundary of the law – and sometimes crossing it – from today it will be the hunts that will have a legal tightrope to tread.

'Unbelievable isn't it? All of a sudden, it's like we are the sheriff's posse and it's the other side who have become the outlaws,' said Dave Wetton, a veteran among 'the antis' who joined the Hunt Saboteurs' Association in April 1964, a few months after its formation.

'Basically, we've won. After 40 years, that takes some getting used to. From now on, we have to accept that we'll have more of a monitoring role – that we'll be hunt crime watchers. There should be no need

By David Sapsted

for sabbing if the hunters behave themselves.'

Nathan Brown, a spokesman for the association, accepts that 'covert surveillance' with video cameras will now become a primary role for the saboteurs. 'We don't trust the hunting fraternity,' he said. 'If they are not being monitored, they will just keep on hunting.'

> **'If hunts really do stop killing animals, then we'll move on. Shooting still goes on. We've been sabotaging shoots for years but that might well get more attention once the killing of foxes stops'**

Since Parliament decided to outlaw hunting with dogs, there has been a marked thinning of saboteurs' ranks and, coincidentally or not, a concomitant drop in the number of acts of vandalism directed at hunt members.

Mr Wetton, 61, believes that, even in their new-found role of monitors, there could still be violence. 'We are like red rags to a bull to the terrier boys,' he said. 'And the people who follow the hunts round in the Toyotas and on quad bikes will be out for revenge because they thought we'd never get the ban.'

But what now for the saboteurs? Aubrey Thomas, 47, a director of the association, said that 'normal' activity would continue until the season ended in a few weeks' time.

'We'll keep turning up but we'll be there with more video cameras. We have no illusions about how successfully the police will be able to control the hunts' activities. I've been trying to keep up with them for 32 years and know how difficult it is.

'If hunts really do stop killing animals, then we'll move on. Shooting still goes on. We've been sabotaging shoots for years but that might well get more attention once the killing of foxes stops. As for fishing, it's an individual thing. The association has never organised any activities against anglers.'

Mr Thomas said that he greeted the arrival of the ban with mixed emotions. 'Last weekend, I was quite euphoric,' he said. 'But a few years ago, a friend lost his life in a hunt protest. On Friday, I don't think I'll celebrate. I'll go and put some flowers on his grave instead.'

For other saboteurs the ban marks what they hope will prove to be the successful end of a long struggle. 'If the hunts really do stop killing foxes, then it will all have been worthwhile,' said a young female saboteur from East Kent. 'I hope it works out that way – I really would like to be able to have a lie-in on a Saturday morning.'

■ This article first appeared in *The Daily Telegraph*, 18 February 2005.
© *Telegraph Group Limited, London 2005*

Hunts intend to push new law to the limit

By Charles Clover,
Environment Editor, and
Catriona Davies

Hunts intend to test police willingness to enforce the ban on hunting with hounds in the remaining three weeks of the season, sources close to the Countryside Alliance said on 21 February 2005.

After a largely law-abiding start to the ban on Saturday, some hunts are expected to defy the ban away from the media scrutiny, particularly in areas where police have expressed unwillingness to waste time following them.

Other hunts are planning to exploit loopholes in the law, such as the use of falconry, for which the number of hounds that may flush out prey species is not limited by the Hunting Act.

Some hunt supporters are planning to defy the police to arrest them for illegal events, such as mouse hunts, which they think will make the law look absurd.

Animal rights campaigners, annoyed by the total of nearly 100 foxes killed by 250 hunts and the appearance of 300,000 hunt supporters on Saturday, warned that hunts risked seeing the ban tightened if they continued to test the law.

Penny Little, a member of Protect Our Wild Animals, who monitored the Bicester hunt, said that if hunts continued to probe for loopholes the Government would close them.

Ms Little said she saw the 'gratuitous, spiteful killing of foxes', which may well have broken the law.

'If the hunting fraternity go out into the field and commit offences and attempt to run circles around this law, there is only one development that can occur, and that is a tightening of the law,' she said.

Speaking on BBC1's *Breakfast with Frost*, she added: 'It will not be repealed because they have behaved in a thuggish and cruel manner.'

However, the Countryside Alliance said hunt supporters had found 'creative' ways to operate within the law.

Some 91 foxes were killed, much the same as on a typical day before the ban, but most were flushed out and shot legally. Some were shot so their scent could be used for drag hunting, and a few were killed accidentally by dogs.

Some hunts said they were merely exercising their dogs.

Many of the 270 hunts that met enjoyed a carnival atmosphere, with thousands meeting to watch the huntsmen depart, or to cheer them through towns and villages.

Supporters said every horse fit for hunting was out, with many brought out of retirement, and 'hirelings' – horses hired for the day – booked up months in advance.

'You couldn't get a horse for love or money,' said Tim Bonner, of the Countryside Alliance. 'It was almost certainly the biggest day's hunting in history.'

He said the number of supporters on Saturday dwarfed last year's Boxing Day turnout of 275,000, which in turn was more than the usual Boxing Day attendance of 200,000 to 250,000. An ordinary Saturday would usually attract about 100,000.

Mr Bonner said: 'Last Thursday, when most hunts had their last legal meet, was a sad day. But on Saturday people came out fighting.

'We are creative people and will find ways to make sure hunting survives until the legislation is repealed.'

The League Against Cruel Sports sent monitors to 100 hunts, and the 'overwhelming majority' found nothing amiss. However, six monitors and other members of the public said they had video evidence of illegal activities.

These will be sent to the league, which will ask lawyers to consider whether they include evidence to be passed to the police.

A few separate complaints were made to police. The only arrests under the law were that of four men in Wiltshire at 4am on Saturday with four dogs and a hare carcass.

However, they were suspected of poaching and released on police bail.

© Telegraph Group Limited, London 2005

Animal rights

Information from Animal Aid

Defending animals does not mean caring abut them more than people. It's about protecting other species from cruelty and unfair treatment and not causing them any harm.

Being interested in animal rights doesn't make you a wimp or a weirdo! Wanting to stop suffering is something of which you should be proud. Going veggie or vegan, not buying certain products because they've been tested on animals and saying you don't want to go to the zoo or a circus with animals are all important ways in which you can help make this world a kinder place. Never let anyone make you feel like you are in the wrong. Always remember that the animals don't have a voice – they need you to speak up for them!

What rights do animals need?

Obviously, animals do not need exactly the same rights as people. For example, the right to vote in elections would be useless to a parrot! But the right to freedom, the right to exercise without being imprisoned or tortured are as important to animals as they are to us.

Why care about animals?

Today it is recognised that animals, just like humans, experience happiness, sadness, fear, physical pain, anger and boredom. We know that they usually enjoy the company of their own kind; that there is a close bond between mothers and their young; that young animals enjoy and learn from play; and that they develop friendships. They have needs, just like people do.

Are people more intelligent?

Animals can't play the piano or pilot a plane – but neither can lots of people! And animals can do some amazing things that are beyond human beings. Can you swing through the trees like an orang-utan? Or sniff out a bone 100 yards away like the average dog? Calling it 'instinct' doesn't make it any less amazing. Anyway, deciding how to treat other creatures on the grounds of their intelligence is wrong. You wouldn't want your rights to be decided by how well you did in your exams, would you?

Can animals communicate?

Anyone with a pet/companion animals will have had first-hand experience of the range of emotions animals can feel and the ways in which they express them. They use sounds and other signals, such as body language, to 'talk' to each other – to attract a new mate, to express contentment or to warn each other of danger. Some animals, such as whales, are able to communicate over vast distances in ways that we don't fully understand.

Do animals feel pain?

Have you ever heard of an animal who could be cut by a knife or burnt by a flame and not feel it? If you kick dogs, they will yelp and cower. If you tread on cats' tails, they'll meow and run off. Whether in your home, or a factory farm, in a laboratory, in captivity or in the wild – animals experience pain and fear and will try to protect themselves from being hurt. This is as true of fish as of monkeys. Even where we cannot be certain that animals experience pain – for example, in the case of worms or insects – we should give them the benefit of the doubt and not cause deliberate harm.

How do we abuse animals?

Millions of animals suffer pain and misery because of humans:

- We slaughter them for food
- We experiment on them in laboratories
- We take the skins off their backs and wear them as shoes, coats and leather jackets
- We hunt them for fun
- We abandon 'pets' that we no longer want
- We keep them in cages in zoos and circuses
- We pollute and destroy their natural habitats

Human rights and animal rights

Similar excuses to those given for treating animals badly were once used to defend the exploitation of certain people. Children were forced to work in mines and as chimney sweeps until society realised that it was unacceptable. Women were not allowed to vote in elections until, after years of campaigning, their rights were recognised. Slaves suffered abuse, humiliation and cruelty and were worked to the point of collapse, even death, because their 'owners' argued that the slaves didn't deserve justice or equality, being of a different race. Is it so far-fetched to compare their fate with that of

Have you ever heard of an animal who could be cut by a knife or burnt by a flame and not feel it? If you kick dogs, they will yelp and cower

animals today? Alice Walker, the well-known African-American writer, once said: 'Animals of the world exist for their own reason. They were not made for humans any more than black people were made for whites or women for men.'

In 1948, the world's nations joined together to issue the Universal Declaration of Human Rights, which states that all people should have freedom and respect whatever their colour, gender, religion or race. Those who believe in animal rights believe animals deserve similar protection. The fact that there is still a great deal of human suffering does not mean that we shouldn't try to help animals, too.

■ The above information is an extract from *Animals & Us*, a publication from Animal Aid. For further information visit their website at www.animalaid.org.uk

© Animal Aid

Animal cruelty law

Animal cruelty law to protect goldfish and dogs' tails

By Charles Clover, Environment Editor

Goldfish could be banned as prizes at fairs and children under 16 prohibited from buying pets under a draft animal welfare Bill published on 14 July 2004.

Ministers believe children under 16 are not mature enough to be responsible for the duty of care needed to protect pets.

The Bill also imposes a ban on 'mutilations', such as the docking of dogs' tails – with exceptions only where there are welfare or management reasons.

There will be a new duty of care on pet owners, including the directors of companies, to look after animals properly. For the first time the law will define what constitutes cruelty. Pet owners and farmers convicted of failing in their duty of care may be disqualified from owning animals.

An animal's welfare is defined as consisting of a suitable environment in which to live, adequate food and water, the ability to display normal behaviour, housing with its own species and appropriate treatment for pain or disease.

Government inspectors and the police are to be given wide-ranging powers to enter premises and vehicles and to confiscate pets to enforce these standards.

Ben Bradshaw, the junior environment minister, said he hoped the Bill would lead to less cruelty and fewer prosecutions. 'What this Bill does not do – and I am someone who regularly empties his slug trap – is fine people £30,000 for stepping on a snail or for killing a slug,' he said. 'It applies to vertebrates only, not to animals in the wild and only to animals kept by people.'

The new measure 'sends a message that buying a pet or owning a pet is an act of responsibility'.

Mr Bradshaw added: 'If you win a goldfish at a fair you are not necessarily thinking through the consequences of having to look after it. You might not have a tank. A lot of goldfish that are won at fairs end up on the compost heap.

'There was a feeling, not least among responsible animal keepers and animal owners, that more needs to be done to prevent cruelty happening in the first place and to encourage responsible pet ownership.

'If a dog or a horse is tethered for a considerable length of time, it is not actually suffering through the

tethering but it is being kept in a way which will lead to suffering, if action isn't taken.

'This is a Bill about prevention. One of the reasons I hope it will be welcomed is that it is far better to intervene to stop an animal being kept in a way that will lead to its suffering than to wait until it has suffered.'

MPs on the Commons environment, food and rural affairs committee are to carry out pre-legislative scrutiny of the draft Bill.

Tim Greet, president of the British Veterinary Association, said: 'With current legislation on cruelty to animals [the Protection of Animals Act 1911] nearly a century old, this major review is certainly not before time.'

While welcoming the proposed legislation, the Kennel Club were 'disappointed' that the draft bill imposed a ban on the docking of dogs' tails.

A spokesman said: 'An outright ban would be detrimental to certain working dogs like spaniels or gun dogs as the dog's tail could get damaged and have to be amputated, which would cause more pain than if it was done when it was first born.'

© Telegraph Group Limited, London 2005

Do your duty

25 reasons for a new animal welfare law

Summary

The aim of the RSPCA is to prevent cruelty and promote kindness to animals. The society has strived to achieve these aims since its inception 180 years ago at a time when there was scant animal welfare law. Although it became an offence to beat, kick or ill-treat some animals such as horses, sheep or cattle in 1822, dog fighting, bear-baiting and bull fighting were not banned until 1835 and there was no specific law against cruelty to all domestic and captive animals until 1911.

The protection of Animals Act 1911 remains the key piece of legislation that the RSPCA relies on as a last resort to prosecute people who treat animals cruelly. The bedrock of the RSPCA's function is, and always has been, educating, advising and raising awareness of animal welfare to prevent cruelty.

Current law

Sadly, current laws require evidence of animal suffering for the cruelty offence to be committed. Even though the animal is likely to suffer unless veterinary treatment is sought or the standard of care is raised, nothing can be done until suffering starts. This causes great frustration for RSPCA inspectors across England and Wales and members of the public. The RSPCA receives thousands of calls every year about animals in worrying conditions including dogs kept in gardens in filth and squalor or horses tethered in unsuitable surroundings in danger of becoming tangled or injured. For the caller reporting the scenario, they often believe that it is a clear-cut case for RSPCA intervention and they understandably become distressed when the Society cannot act because the dog or horse is not yet suffering. These cases can and do lead to suffering when advice is ignored. RSPCA inspectors have had the frustration of repeating visits up

to 25 times before the animal has deteriorated to the point where there is evidence of suffering that is required by law.

Time to act

The RSPCA wants to act on the early warning signs of animal neglect. The government-proposed Animal Welfare Bill would facilitate this process with the new welfare offence.

---

25 reasons for a new animal welfare law

Here are the key areas in which the RSPCA believes changes to the law will have the most significant impact on animal welfare. *Do your duty* explains how the RSPCA believes the bill affects each area and details where the bill does not go far enough.

1. Welfare offence
2. Cruelty ofence
3. Fighting and baiting
4. Animal tethering
5. Animal mutilations
6. Goads and electric training devices
7. Pet purchasing by children
8. Animals as prizes
9. Riding establishments
10. Livery yards
11. Pet fairs
12. Exotic animals
13. Pet shops and pet sales
14. Circuses
15. Animal sanctuaries
16. Dog registration
17. Boarding establishments
18. Breeding establishments
19. Stray animal welfare
20. Farmed animals
21. Traps
22. Penalties
23. Time limits for prosecutions
24. Disqualification orders
25. Deprivation orders.

The Society applauds the premise of the bill that those responsible for animals have a statutory duty to ensure their welfare – a 'duty of care'. This will allow authorities to point to legally recognised welfare standards on occasions where conditions are found to be inadequate. If advice to raise welfare standards to the legal minimum is ignored, criminal proceedings could be taken. A welfare offence would carry a lesser penalty than the penalty for the cruelty offence and the animals will have been saved from suffering.

Introduction

Today's laws to protect animals from cruelty and suffering have barely changed since 1911 when the streets were full of horsedrawn carts and women were refused the right to vote.

Nearly 100 years after the Protection of Animals Act 1911 came into force, RSPCA inspectors are still having to walk away from situations where an animal's welfare is being compromised and wait until there is evidence of suffering before any action can be taken.

Dealing with cruelty

RSPCA inspectors are fully trained in all aspects of animal welfare and the law. In responding to each call of neglect or cruelty, RSPCA inspectors will make a careful judgement about whether or not advice can rectify the problem. In some cases they will give those responsible for an animal a verbal or written warning if they feel the guidance may be ignored. Where it is considered that criminal proceedings should be taken to present further suffering to the animal, RSPCA inspectors prepare a case for the Society's legal team to consider. Inspectors often work with the police or local authorities to assist with this procedure.

Staggering statistics

In 2003, the RSPCA received 1,279,953 calls including requests for

---

welfare advice, reports of injured or trapped animals, or reports of suspected neglect or suffering. Of the 105,932 complaints of suspected cruelty, 50 per cent resulted in advice being given to improve standards of welfare. Verbal warnings were given in 4,070 instances due to concerns that an offence would be committed if advice was not followed immediately.

The RSPCA believes that education is the most effective way to raise animal welfare and it will only initiate criminal proceedings as a last resort. Careful consideration is given before taking a prosecution. The RSPCA is a private prosecutor, it is not a public authority and it has no statutory power to prosecute. However, the inspectors' training in 'evidence gathering' and the RSPCA's use of the Code for Crown Prosecutors* in deciding whether to bring a prosecution results in a high success rate where prosecutions are necessary.

The effectiveness of education is being demonstrated through the Society's new welfare assessment scheme. Where an animal's welfare is being compromised, inspectors provide those responsible for an animal with written guidance on how to improve standards of care. In the scheme's first year (June 2003 to May 2004) 2,661 people received advice and the majority followed it. Sadly 315 people ignored the advice given and although the welfare concerns remain the RSPCA is powerless to act.

A kinder future

The government's draft Animal Welfare Bill aims to pull together and reform more than 20 pieces of animal welfare legalisation into one modernised law to prevent suffering.

The Society believes the welfare offence in the Animal Welfare Bill will help to tackle the problem of basic welfare not being provided. It will require owners of captive animals to take reasonable steps to meet their animals' welfare needs in an appropriate manner and those needs will include:

■ the need for a suitable environment

■ the need for adequate food and water
■ the need for protection from pain, injury and disease
■ the need to exhibit normal behaviour

The need for protection from fear and distress should also be included, although the current draft does not do this.

The RSPCA believes animal owners and keeps have a duty to find out about their animals and most people already do this. However, the RSPCA also supports the idea that the welfare offence should be supported by government codes of practice. These should contain guidance on what to do to deliver appropriate welfare standards. In many instances where welfare is being compromised, the owners is unaware of their mistake(s). The codes of practice should be widely available and serve as an education tool.

Where the welfare offence may have been committed, authorities investigating reports of neglect will be able to explain the welfare problem by reference to the relevant code of practice and provide an opportunity for the animal owner to remedy the situation. If the advice is ignored, proceedings could be taken under the new welfare offence as a last resort to prevent animal suffering.

* The code for Crown Prosecutors sets out the basic principles Crown Prosecutors should follow when they make case decisions.

■ The above information is an extract from the RSPCA's report *Do Your Duty*. For further information visit their website: www.rspca.org.uk

© RSPCA

Comparison with other bodies taking prosecutions

	Success rate for RSPCA prosecutions*	Success rate for all (including RSPCA) animal cruelty prosecutions*
1998	95.6%	79%
1999	97.2%	77.6%
2000	96.9%	77.6%
2001	94.3%	75.3%
2002	96%	75.8%
2003	96.6%	Not available

* Data taken from RSPCA annnual reports and answers to parliamentary question given by Rt Hon Keith Bradley (*Hansard*, 15 January 2002, col 182W) and Mr Bob Ainsworth (*Hansard*, 6 March 2003, col 1224W)

Source: RSPCA

Fashion's new F-word

By Helen Weathers

Ten years ago, it would have been unthinkable. Supermodels and designers giving the animal rights lobby the fashion equivalent of a two-fingered salute by embracing fur with gusto.

Fur, once the dirty word of fashion, is back with a vengeance and, apparently, without a guilty conscience. Mink and chinchilla are making a brazen reappearance on the catwalk and women who previously wouldn't be seen dead wearing a dead animal are draping themselves in pelts.

This new mood of defiance couldn't have been more apparent than when Mick Jagger's model daughter Elizabeth, 20, opened London Fashion Week by wearing a Julien Macdonald fox stole, strutting down a catwalk strewn with cowhide.

And she wasn't the only one. A veritable farm of luxurious furs went into Macdonald's collection, heralding what fashion writers say will be *the* big trend for 2005/6.

After the show, Macdonald – a favourite of Kylie Minogue and Joely Richardson – gushed 'I adore fur; it adds ultimate luxury and glamour to my collections', while stressing he uses only animal farms which follow international rules and regulations.

The lobby group PETA (People For the Ethical Treatment of Animals) – which famously brought us the slogan 'I'd rather go naked than wear fur' and persuaded the world's supermodels to pose in nothing but their birthday suits for an anti-fur campaign – is, understandably, far from happy.

'By wearing fur, Elizabeth Jagger is endorsing hideous cruelty to animals,' says PETA campaign coordinator Jodi Ruckley.

'But in no way is this show an indication that wearing fur is becoming more acceptable for most women. It will never be acceptable because animal suffering will always be unacceptable. A recent survey for *Cosmopolitan* magazine showed that 91 per cent of women would never wear fur, despite what is happening on the catwalk.

'This is just about a designer trying to get into the papers by being provocative. I don't think dressing models like cavemen is particularly sophisticated or intelligent.'

> *Fur, once the dirty word of fashion, is back with a vengeance and, apparently, without a guilty conscience*

Certainly there are still designers – including Calvin Klein, Ralph Lauren, Stella McCartney, Moschino and Vivienne Westwood – who refuse to use fur on principle.

And there are a raft of celebrities who support PETA, including Hollywood actresses Charlize Theron, Drew Barrymore, Hilary Swank, Jennifer Aniston, Angelina Jolie and Natalie Portman, as well as supermodel Christy Turlington, who appeared in the original 'I'd rather go naked' poster.

But what of supermodels Naomi Campbell and Cindy Crawford, who joined her in the PETA campaign?

Celebrities pose for PETA

Campbell, who was recently criticised for modelling a three-quarter-length mink coat, also appeared at Julien Macdonald's show, but wisely steered clear of fur.

'Naomi was once so anti-fur. In 1994, when she was part of the PETA campaign and we showed her videos of animals in fur farms, she cried and said she couldn't believe it,' says Andrew Butler, one of PETA's campaign co-ordinators.

'But just a few years later, she went back on her word. She was offered money to wear fur and she accepted.'

As for Cindy Crawford, she sparked controversy in December when she starred in a mink coat advert for American fashion house *Blackglama*.

Her publicist explained the volte-face by saying Cindy never really supported PETA's stand against fur, but was being 'really nice' to them by lending her image to their campaign.

And Cindy is not alone in being seduced by the allure of fur. Increasingly, celebrities are becoming bolder about wearing animal pelts. Gone, it seems, are the days when *American Vogue* editor-in-chief Anna Wintour was assaulted with a frozen raccoon because of her love of fur and activists showered the front row of a Marc Jacobs catwalk show with a bucket of maggots.

In recent times, supermodel Kate Moss has been photographed wearing a vintage coyote coat, Lady Helen Taylor has worn black mink, Jade Jagger has wrapped up in a designer silver fox coat and Ivana Trump has plumped for chinchilla.

J-Lo last week bagged the prestigious final slot in New York fashion week with her debut show and caused controversy by using lots of fur.

One British fashion editor commented after the show: 'It's bad enough that fur is so dominant in fashion this season. But when Jennifer Lopez endorses it, she's telling the world she thinks it's cool.

'If J-Lo thinks it's cool, then so will the millions of kids who idolise her.'

However, not everyone in the fashion industry feels the same. They see the renaissance of fur as long overdue and rail at the aggressive tactics of animal activists who shame consumers into not wearing it.

'At Fendi, fur was never out. We have never stopped using it and have always treated it as the most luxurious fabric,' says designer Carla Fendi.

'People say fur is back because women want the freedom to wear whatever they want.'

Despite the frozen raccoon episode, Anna Wintour has not changed her views on fur in the slightest.

'It is undoubtedly the number one fashion accessory this season,' she says.

> **While the wealthy women who buy designer furs see only luxury and beauty, animal rights activists see dead animals which have led short, miserable, painful lives**

'And I'm not just talking about a traditional fur coat. There's fur trim on sweaters, coats, even dresses.'

These endorsements have been seized on by the International Fur Trade Federation, which talks soothingly of how the industry has invested major sums into scientific advice on animal welfare, farming and trapping techniques.

Its justification is that fur has been traded for thousands of years and is vital to the livelihoods of many aboriginal communities.

It reels off a list of more than 300 designers who have recently used fur, including some of fashion's biggest names: Oscar de la Renta, Dolce & Gabbana, Fendi, Gianfranco Ferre, Michael Kors, Karl Lagerfeld, Yves St Laurent, Valentino, Versace, Givenchy, Zandra Rhodes, Christian Lacroix, Donna Karan, Jean Paul Gaultier and Sonia Rykiel.

While the wealthy women who buy designer furs see only luxury and beauty, animal rights activists see dead animals which have led short, miserable, painful lives.

'People often say when they wear vintage furs "Oh it's old, it's been dead a long time" as a way to make themselves feel less guilty,' says Andrew Butler of PETA.

'But they are still advertising cruelty. Minks are very small animals – you need 60 to 80 for just one coat.

'They are gassed to death by piling them into a chamber. We believe that some are still alive and conscious when they are skinned because there are farms that won't pay out the money for the proper equipment.

'Mink spend their entire life in wire cages. It causes psychosis, self-mutilation and cannibalism.'

> **While Britain's attitude to fur remains largely dominated by conscience, the markets in Europe, the US and Russia are booming**

But these grim details are not stopping the new rush for fur. According to the International Fur Trade Federation, more than one million people are employed fulltime in the industry and sales worldwide total £6 billion a year.

While Britain's attitude to fur remains largely dominated by conscience – though thanks to the celebrities recently seen draped in furs, that may be changing – the markets in Europe, the US and Russia are booming.

London's top stores Harvey Nichols, Selfridges and Harrods do not stock fur.

A spokesperson for Harvey Nichols, which has not sold fur for ten years, says: 'Fur is a very important trend on the catwalks, but our buyers are good at working around it.'

But for how long? PETA's latest campaign slogan is 'Fur is dead', but in the fickle world of fashion, that will not deter some people.

■ This article first appeared in *The Daily Mail*, 15 February 2005.
© 2005 Associated Newspapers Ltd

The facts about the fur trade

Information from Advocates for Animals

How many animals are killed by the fur trade each year?

Every year, over 50 million animals are killed so that their fur can be used by the fashion industry; that's more than 130,000 animals slaughtered every day just so that someone else can wear their coats. Worldwide, more than 30 million animals are bred and killed on intensive fur farms with a further 20 million trapped and killed in the wild.

The fur industry goes to great lengths to hide the horrendous cruelty involved, but many undercover investigations have produced detailed evidence showing the terrible suffering of these animals, both in the way they are kept and in the way they are killed.

How did fur farming originate?

As wild populations of fur-bearing animals declined and disappeared due to trapping, animals were caught live in order to breed them in captivity. This originated in Canada at the beginning of the 20th century. Today, fur farms can be found across the world, with large numbers in Scandinavia, Russia and the USA.

Which animals are bred for their fur?

The two species most commonly bred for their fur are the North American mink and the arctic fox, although other animals including chinchillas, raccoons and rabbits are also used.

How are the animals kept?

Animals are kept in long rows of barren wire cages in open-sided sheds. A typical cage for a mink measures 24" long by 10" wide, whilst an arctic fox will be confined in a cage measuring on average 40" by 40". These barren prisons, scarcely bigger than the animals themselves, are where they will spend their entire lives.

Advocates for Animals

How different is this to their lives in the wild?

In the wild, both mink and foxes are predatory animals with complex behaviour patterns. Mink will roam over territories of up to 3 square kilometres and spend most of their time close to water. Foxes generally live in small family groups and arctic foxes are known to wander hundreds of kilometres from their place of birth. On fur farms the natural instincts of these species are cruelly stifled from being incarcerated in barren cages. The stress and deprivation caused by these conditions often result in the animals performing unnatural repetitive behaviours and can lead to self-mutilation.

Fur farms tend to follow a regular calendar. Animals are mated in February, give birth in May and offspring weaned at 6-7 weeks. Unless they are kept for breeding purposes, most mink and foxes are killed in November at about 7-8 months of age when their pelts are in prime condition.

How are the captive animals killed?

Most mink are killed by gassing or lethal injection. Some are clubbed to death or have their necks broken.

Every year, over 50 million animals are killed so that their fur can be used by the fashion industry

---

Foxes are most commonly electrocuted; one electrode is inserted into the animal's rectum and another into its mouth. The fox generally does not lose consciousness for between one and two minutes, and animals may later revive only to have to then undergo this cruelty again. The main reason for selecting these killing methods is to ensure that the fur is not damaged. Those carrying out the killing need no training or qualifications.

What about animals caught in the wild?

Millions of the world's most beautiful fur-bearing animals are being systematically trapped and hunted in the wild for their skins. This trade has been responsible for the widespread decline in many species over the past two centuries and has resulted in the extinction of some others, including the sea mink and the Falkland Island fox. Beavers too were almost hunted to extinction in the 19th century until reprieved by a change in fashion.

In more recent times, big cats such as the leopard, tiger and jaguar were in danger of being wiped out until an international appeal succeeded in protecting them from the commercial fur trade. However, few of these animals now remain in the wild and many are endangered. The thick fur of the snow leopard made it popular with the fur trade. In fact there may now be as few as 4,500 of these beautiful animals left in the high mountain regions of central Asia and the Himalayas.

As the larger cat species became more scarce and increasingly protected, so the fur trade turned its attention to the smaller cats such as the ocelot, margay, lynx and little-known Geoffrey's cat. These smaller cat species are now being trapped and hunted in large numbers.

How are the wild animals caught?

One of the most commonly used animal traps is the steel-jawed leg-hold trap – a device so barbaric that it was outlawed in Britain during the late 1950s as well as in many other countries. The British ban followed the publication in 1951 of the Scott-Henderson report on *Cruelty to Wild Animals*. The report describes the gin trap – a version of the leg-hold trap used in the UK at the time – as 'a diabolical instrument which causes an incalculable amount of suffering'. Sadly these traps are still commonly used in many countries across the world.

When the trap slams shut on the leg or paw of its victim, the jaws of the trap bite deeply into the animal's flesh. The animal may be left in agony for several days until the trapper arrives to inspect his catch. The trapped animal will go to desperate lengths to free itself from the steel jaws, often attempting to gnaw off its trapped limb; it is estimated that up to one in four trapped animals chews off its own foot to escape, only to then die from blood loss or infection.

What other methods are used?

The two other common trapping methods used are the Conibear and the snare. The Conibear trap is sometimes referred to by the fur trade as an 'instant kill trap', although this is not always the case, and in a 1975 interview, Conibear admitted his trap's failings, stating that 'some animals . . . will suffer a lingering death'. Like the leg-hold trap, neither the Conibear nor the snare can discriminate and all too often animals are trapped, often with severe injuries, for hours or even days in indescribable agony. For every wild animal killed for its fur at least three others are caught, killed and discarded. Known as 'trash' animals by the fur trade, they include squirrels, rabbits, woodchuck, sheep and deer as well as pet cats and dogs.

How quickly do the animals die when caught by these methods?

Some animals that are trapped will die from their injuries, in acute pain or from starvation. Those that survive until the trapper returns are usually beaten to death or simply stood or stomped on; bullets are not used to kill trapped animals because they damage the fur. A graphic account of the death of a trapped animal was given at a US Congressional hearing:

'Suddenly the club smashed across the coyote's nose and slammed him to the ground. But the blow was not delivered with precision. Almost instantly he was in a semi-crouch; blood spurting from the nose, eyes dazed. Again the club fell. The trapper, with one practised motion, grabbed the stunned coyote by the hind legs, stretching the animal full length while planting his foot heavily on its neck. The other foot delivered a series of thumping blows to the coyote's chest expelling hollow gasps of air. Releasing the hind legs, the trapper rested one foot on the coyote's neck, the other on the chest. The coyote's eyes bulged, the mouth gaped, the tongue hung listlessly along the blood-stained jaw. Periodically stomping near the heart, the trapper maintained this position for 14 minutes . . . Satisfied the coyote was dead, the trapper added several final stomps.'

How can the fur trade possibly defend these barbaric methods?

In an attempt to allay public concern over the cruelty of trapping and to

stave off bans on the use of certain traps, the fur trade has funded what it euphemistically calls 'humane trap research'. One example of this work is an experiment to discover how long it takes animals such as beaver, mink and musk-rat to drown. Animals were put into traps and held under water whilst their death-throes were observed and monitored. The results were horrifying. The 'average' beaver struggled for 9.5 minutes whilst it was 25 minutes before the heart of one of the animals stopped beating. Yet the fur trade argues that drowning is a humane method of killing.

Surely garments made from such barbaric methods cannot be sold in the UK?

In Scotland, fur farming was banned in 2002, and in England and Wales in 2003. However, furs from animals farmed abroad can still be sold in the UK. Although the use of steel-jawed leg-hold traps to catch wild animals was banned in the UK in 1958, the importation of skins and garments produced from animals caught in leg-hold traps is legal. Also, in the UK, wild animals can still legally be snared or caught in other traps.

What other countries have a ban on fur farming?

Some European countries have taken steps to restrict, phase out or ban fur farming. For example in Switzerland, stringent legislation prevents cage-rearing of animals and, in the Netherlands, farming of foxes and chinchillas has been banned. Surveys in countries around the world have repeatedly shown public opposition to the fur trade.

A comprehensive study in 2001 by the European Union on 'The welfare of animals kept for fur' concluded that the typical fox or mink cage does not provide for the most important basic needs of the animals. Despite this, approximately 70% of all fur is still produced in Europe.

■ The above information is from Advocates for Animal's website which can be found at www.advocatesforanimals.org.uk
© *Advocates for Animals*

International fur trade today

Information from the International Fur Trade Federation (IFTF)

Introduction

The fur trade is unique among modern industries in supporting a remarkable range of cultures, traditional skills and lifestyles. It also plays an important role in environmental conservation and habitat management – as well as contributing to international business, providing employment and economic benefits to many countries.

Man and fur

Man has always used the products of other species, and most people recognise our right to do so provided we behave responsibly and with respect, and ensure that natural productivity and habitats are not damaged. Modern society feels a particular impulse to ensure that the animals we use, whether for food, clothing, medical research, sport or pets, are treated humanely and with consideration. The fur industry, whilst rejecting the attempts by 'animal rights' campaigners to penalise people who wish to wear fur, has long recognised that farming and trapping techniques must take account of the scientific advice on welfare – and has invested major sums in research to this end.

Though necessarily expensive, fur remains a supreme example of a fashion product that derives from a wholly natural sustainable resource, is long-lasting but ultimately biodegradable, delivers rare benefits in sustaining fragile communities and habitats, and which embodies traditions of human craftsmanship that few other modern products possess.

History

Fur has been traded for thousands of years, and the need to satisfy growing demand explains key developments in modern history. Furs were traded by the Phoenicians and other ancient

Mediterranean civilisations. The search for fine skins (including sable) lay behind Russia's push eastwards in the 17th century, beyond the Urals into Siberia and the Pacific regions. The early history of North America turns around the commercial need to satisfy European demand, initially for beaver, leading to intense competition between French and English adventurers, traders and eventually governments.

Aboriginal Americans caught and supplied the furs for this trade, and sold food and supplies to the traders. The fur trade was one of the few sectors of the European economy in which aboriginal hunters could participate while maintaining – and reinforcing – their traditional lifestyle and cultural values.

Even today – and marking the strong link with history that characterises many aspects of fur – the trade is important for the livelihoods of many aboriginal Canadians, Alaskans, 'Cajun' Louisianans and Siberians. Many areas supportive of fur-bearing species are unsuited to agricultural development, and a bush-oriented lifestyle remains a viable, and sometimes the only, economic alternative. About one-half of Canada's 80,000 trappers are aboriginals – Indians, Metis or Inuit.

Fur, conservation and wildlife management

The use of wild species for fur is strictly controlled, both nationally and internationally. The international fur trade uses no endangered species.

The commercial demand for fur, and government regulation of trapping, have in fact ensured that trappers are effectively the modern world's eyes and ears in monitoring the ecology and environment of sensitive areas. Trapping communities, participating in scientific wildlife management programmes, use trapping to control animal overpopulation problems, avoiding imbalances that can bring disease and damage to both animal populations and their natural habitats. In many instances, commercially

harvested fur-bearing populations are more stable and abundant today than 100 years ago – whilst the threat to other species endangered by poaching, habitat reduction, intensive agriculture and encroachment by rival species continues to cause concern.

The Convention on International Trade in Endangered Species (CITES) which regulates trade in threatened and endangered species and the World Conservation Union (also known as the IUCN – of which IFTF is a member) are both important international conservation organisations. They seek to conserve the world's natural resources and ensure through international co-operation that man's use of them is sustainable. The international fur trade, through the IFTF, works closely with both organisations.

Trapping

Trappers, who have a commitment to their own habitat and to a responsible use of wildlife that goes back many generations, energetically support current humane-trap research programmes designed to ensure the highest possible standards of animal care – in contrast to the urban-based 'animal rights' industry which, while raising large sums from the public for its 'campaigns', has contributed nothing to research into trap improvements that can bring genuine improvements in animal welfare. Such research has been financed by the fur industry itself, in co-operation with the Canadian and US governments.

Fur farming

Farmed furs (mink and fox) are the mainstay of the fur trade, accounting for approximately 85 per cent of the industry's turnover. Most fur farming takes place in Northern Europe (66 per cent) and North America (13 per cent of mink). The remainder occurs in countries as far apart as Argentina, the Baltic States, China, the Ukraine and Russia. Fur farming is a well-regulated farming activity.

Traditional skills live on

European furriers have been organised in guilds, since at least the

---

The fur trade is unique among modern industries in supporting a remarkable range of cultures, traditional skills and lifestyles

---

14th century. For many centuries, furriers made caps, gloves, muffs, collars and linings for cloaks and coats. But it was only in the 19th century that fur garments were worn showing the hair on the outside.

Many skills are involved in the transformation of fur from pelt to luxury garment. Before pelts come to auction they are scraped and dried to prevent decay. They can then be stored safely.

Pelts must be dressed, which is a highly skilled operation. At the dresser, skins are soaked several times in tubs or tanks in brine or saline solutions to clean and soften them. Skin layers and other tissues are then removed. This is followed by placing the skins in a 'drum' (known as a 'kicker') for further softening. The skins are then 'pickled', placed in a tanning bath where chrome is added, and then dried. Afterwards, skins are stretched and, if no dyeing is required, the goods are finished by ironing or hand combing and often plasticising to bring out the true lustre.

If skins are dyed, blended or reinforced, modern scientific techniques, often combined with further plucking or shearing, can transform furs into a multitude of colours, from conventional dark to very light pastel shades, and different textures. After processing, pelts are sorted and matched. Then, according to the designer's pattern, they are wetted, stretched and tacked to a blocking table, where the furrier works to shape and soften them. In many cases the pelts are let out (sliced) into narrow strips and then stitched back together using hundreds of intricate seams, in order to make a flowing, supple material – a technique demanding painstaking skill. Off-cuts are not discarded, but sewn to make 'plates' which are then used to make less expensive garments or linings. As

every pelt is unique, the making of fur garments can never be automated. The trade is still characterised by small-scale family-run businesses of specialist craftsmen. It can take months to produce a fine coat from the raw material to the finished product.

The fur trade today

Fur is an international business today, adding value to many different economies on its journey from its origins to luxury shops of North America, the Far East and Europe.

Auction

Pelts normally enter the international trading system through one of the modern international auction houses located, traditionally, close to producing areas. The world's largest auction houses are in Copenhagen, Helsinki, Oslo, Saint Petersburg, Seattle and Toronto. The farmers and trappers who ship the raw skins to the auction houses – either direct or through local collectors – receive the price paid at auction less a small commission for grading and handling.

The buyers at auctions need to exercise high levels of skill, experience and commercial acumen in selecting and bidding for the furs, which are traditionally sold in graded and assorted 'lots'. Buyers may be furriers buying in their own right, but are more likely to be brokers using their skills to buy on behalf of furriers, or dealers whose companies sell finished skins to furriers or manufacturers around the world. Fur wholesalers and merchants, buying at auction to supply manufacturers, operate as truly international enterprises and hold stocks in North America, London and the Far East. The high value and volume of the skins handled means that entrepôt trade can have a high economic impact in countries which are not, in themselves, traditionally large markets for finished furs, for example the United Kingdom.

Manufacture

The auction houses release the skins to the buyer after payment. After dressing, the skins will then make a further journey to the furrier or manufacturer, often working to the patterns of world-famous designers. Important furriery skills still operate close to traditional markets, such as the USA, Canada, Greece, France, Germany, Austria, Italy and the Nordic countries. But many top quality garments are nowadays also made in Hong Kong and China, drawing on Asian traditions of meticulous craftsmanship and attention to detail. (Indeed, Northern China has nurtured a tradition of finishing skins and creating fur garments going back many centuries.)

Markets

Markets for fur garments have traditionally existed in North America, Europe, Russia and the Nordic countries and these remain important. But in recent years sales of furs have greatly expanded in the prospering economies of Japan, Korea and China. Supply and demand fluctuates and can be cyclical, like that for most manufactured products, the main factor being levels of economic confidence – though periods of successive warm winters can also depress sales. 1996 and 1997 saw a major revival, with many markets showing an increase in retail sales.

Fur retailing is traditionally a small, family-run business, often drawing on skills passed down the family through several generations. Large department stores are also important outlets for furs, both for full-fur fashion garments and for pieces using fur as a trim or accessory.

Fur and fashion trends

Fur is clearly in fashion as demonstrated by the fact that sales of fur are on the increase. Moreover, the number of leading designers and/or design houses working in fur, shearling or fur trim has grown impressively over the past five years. They value fur's unique ability to add texture, glamour and sensuality to an ensemble. Over 300 fashion designers are currently working with fur including Oscar de la Renta, Dolce & Gabbana, Fendi, Gianfranco Ferré, Gucci, Michael Kors, Karl Lagerfeld, Yves St Laurent, Valentino and Versace.

Economic impact

The fur industry extends so widely that it is almost impossible to quantify its global economic impact. However, some examples include:

- Over 1 million people are employed full-time by the fur trade worldwide

- Fur sales worldwide totalled some US$ 11 billion in 2001/2
- Some 117,000 enterprises exist worldwide – retailers, dressers, brokers, etc.
- Annual retail fur sales for the US alone were US$ 1.5 billion in 2001/2. The US fur industry comprises approximately 1,400 retailers and 100 manufacturers
- In Canada, the entire fur industry adds some Can$800 million to the Canadian economy annually, employing some 75,000 Canadians in total
- Hong Kong is the world's leading exporter of fur clothing to the value of more than US$230 million annually
- In Denmark, fur farming was worth Euro 514 million in 2002, the country's third largest export after bacon and cheese
- In Finland, the annual fur production value is Euro 250 million, greater than that of beef, with over 50 per cent of fur farmers relying on fur farming as their sole source of income

- The above information is from the International Fur Trade Federation's website: www.iftf.com. All details were correct at time of going to print.
© International Fur Trade Federation (IFTF)

Fur farming

Information from the International Fur Trade Federation (IFTF)

Introduction

Fur farming began in North America in the 19th century, arriving in Europe in the early years of the 20th century. Today, after over 100 years of selective breeding, combined with good nutrition, housing and veterinary care, farmed fur-bearing animals are domesticated and amongst the world's best-cared-for farm animals.

The most common farmed fur-bearing animal is mink, followed by fox. Other species farmed on a smaller scale include nutria, chinchilla, fitch, sable and finn racoon. Most fur farming takes place in Northern Europe (66 per cent) and North

America (13 per cent of mink). The remainder occurs in countries as far apart as Argentina, the Baltic States, China, Ukraine and Russia.

Farmed furs are the mainstay of the fur trade, accounting for some 85 per cent of the industry's turnover. Production figures for mink and fox farming vary annually. Most recent figures (2002) show that approximately 35.5 million pelts were produced in that year (87 per cent mink; 13 per cent fox).

An employment lifeline

Fur farming provides a livelihood for many thousands of individuals in Europe and North America. In Europe, there are some 6,000 fur farms, providing full-time employment to 30,000 individuals. The fur sector as a whole provides some 214,000 full and part-time jobs in the European Union. In North America there are some 760 mink and fox farms (400 in USA and 360 in Canada). Most farms are small family-run businesses. The fur sector as a whole provides some 255,000 full and part-time jobs in North America.

Revenue from fur farming allows many farmers, particularly in Europe, to supplement income from other agricultural activities. Fur farming also allows farming to remain economically viable where climatic conditions limit the options open to farmers in terms of what they can produce and market profitably.

Efficient use for animal by-products

Fur farming provides an efficient use of animal by-products from human food production purchased from fish and poultry processors and other farming sectors. The consumption by fur animals of these by-products, which are not intended for human use, helps to keep down the actual cost of human food production.

A caring sector

Fur farmers have a vested interest in keeping their animals healthy and content. As anyone who owns and cares for fur-bearing animals knows, pet-owners included, the condition of an animal's coat is a key indicator of its well-being. Scientific research into the behaviour and welfare of farmed fur-bearing animals has been ongoing, particularly in the Netherlands, Russia and the Nordic countries, financed by governments and the fur sector.

Fur farming is well regulated and operates within the highest standards of care. In the European Union, Council Directive 98/58 sets down rules covering the welfare of all farmed animals, including fur farmed animals. Directive 93/119 deals with the slaughter and killing of fur and other farmed animals. Additionally, the Council of Europe adopted a Recommendation, revised in 1999, designed to ensure the health and welfare of farmed fur animals. The Recommendation deals comprehensively with matters of animal care, from the farming environment to stockmanship and inspection. Its requirements have been included in the European Fur Breeders' Association (EFBA) Code of Practice. In North America, fur farmers also follow strict Codes of Practice and conform to provincial, state or national animal welfare and other regulations.

Regular veterinary checks are carried out in accordance with industry guidelines, provincial, state or national requirements.

In Russia fur farming is covered by agricultural and company legislation, as well as specific laws on fur animal breeding.

Farming methods

The present housing systems have evolved through independent scientific research (notably behavioural studies), and practical experience over many generations of animals on farms. Mink are generally housed in sheds four metres wide. These sheds are open-sided with roofing panels. They provide normal temperature and light conditions, while protecting against direct sunlight, wind and rain. Wire cages are placed in rows in the sheds. Foxes are housed in similar sheds. In both cases, the cages are raised off the ground to ensure good hygiene. These cages give the farm animals sufficient space for normal movement and investigative behaviour.

Fur farming provides a livelihood for many thousands of individuals in Europe and North America. In Europe, there are some 6,000 fur farms, providing full-time employment to 30,000 individuals

---

In mink farming, year-round nestboxes bedded with straw or wood shavings are provided for breeding purposes and to ensure that the animals sleep and rest comfortably. Research has shown that the provision of a nesting box, which is now standard in mink production, is of great importance to the welfare of farmed mink.

Both mink kits and fox cubs remain in the same cage as their mothers until weaned at the age of 7-8 weeks. After that the animals are housed in little groups of 2-3 through their growth period, and only breeding animals, selected among the mature animals late in the autumn, are housed separately. Non-breeding mature animals are killed quickly and humanely. Methods used are closely controlled under national and European law and North American provincial/state or national requirements. They are administered on the farm thereby minimising the need for stressful transport.

Generally, both mink and fox are fed on a wet feed made from fish, dairy, poultry and other agricultural by-products. This is high in nutrients and may have added supplements to ensure that ideal nutrition levels are provided to maintain good health and well-being. Clean water is available at all times.

What the experts say

'From a scientific point of view, fur animals that have been domesticated for more than ten generations must be considered as so far genetically removed from their ancestors that they have to be treated as fully domesticated subspecies. Irrespective of the present taxonomy of the animals it has to be realised that it would be disastrous to the welfare of the animals to go on treating them as wild animals in respect to legislation. The majority of farmed fur animals require the same status as all other commonly held animals in modern husbandry.'

(Professor Knud Erik Heller, Institute of Population Biology, University of Copenhagen, June 1993)

'There are behavioural problems associated with all forms of animal husbandry, but there are a number of positive sides to fur farming – low frequency of illness, natural outdoor climate, natural light, small farms which allow good contact between farmer and animals, often natural reproduction, close to normal mother/offspring relations and slaughter on the farm.'

(Norwegian Court judgement in favour of fur farming under the Animal Welfare Act – January 2000)

■ Currently, about 2.78 million animals are used in research in the UK each year. (p. 1)

■ Behind the scare stories and myths there lies an ever growing number of successes and advances in the field of human medicine. For many years, humans have been benefited from the healthcare advances that animal-based research has achieved. (p. 3)

■ The total in 2003 rose by 59,000 to 2.79 million, an increase of 2.2 per cent on 2002, the Home Office data showed. (p. 4)

■ All kinds of animals are used, including dogs, cats, horses, monkeys, donkeys, pigs, sheep, hamsters, mice, rats and frogs. (p. 5)

■ Animals are usually selected on the grounds of convenience and cost, the vast majority of animals used being mice and rats, and not on the basis of their 'human similarities'. (p. 6)

■ Genetically modified animals were used in 764,000 regulated procedures representing 27 per cent of all procedures for 2003 (compared with 26 per cent in 2002 and 8 per cent in 1995). (p. 8)

■ A published analysis by the Medical Research Council and industry scientists found that on average animals can predict 70% of the side effects in humans. (p. 9)

■ Each life is precious to the one who is living it – whether animal or human. And because animals have the capacity to suffer, it is wrong to inflict pain on them. (p. 10)

■ Medical research has saved the lives of a quarter of a million children between 1 and 14 in the UK during the past 50 years. (p. 12)

■ The UK's system for regulating animal experiments is the tightest in the world, and is the main restriction on medical advance. (p. 16)

■ Alternatives are already being used in laboratories all around the world, and the European Commission has a scientific centre in Italy for the validation of alternative methods. Still, millions of animal experiments continue. (p. 17)

■ Under the law, the scientists who have the licences to carry out the experiments have the main responsibility for the welfare of the animals in their care. In addition, every licensed laboratory has to have a senior person (the certificate holder) whose job is to ensure that it complies with the law. (p. 18)

■ In an opinion poll taken in December 2002 only 36% of those questioned supported the view that 'hunting should not be allowed to continue at all as cruelty is more important to me than civil liberties'. (p. 20)

■ In areas where coursing takes place, hare populations are generally higher and healthier due to people's interests in preserving their natural habitat. (p. 21)

■ Undercover investigation by the League Against Cruel Sports has revealed that very many foxhunts provide artificial earths in the area in which they hunt, and even provide food for foxes, encouraging them to breed so as to produce more potential quarries for their 'sport'. (p. 22)

■ It may have been (and may continue to be) a long, hard struggle, but the passing of the Hunting Act should be an inspiration to all who continue to fight other forms of cruelty. (p. 24)

■ After a largely law-abiding start to the ban, some hunts are expected to defy the ban away from the media scrutiny, particularly in areas where police have expressed unwillingness to waste time following them. (p. 27)

■ Today it is recognised that animals, just like humans, experience happiness, sadness, fear, physical pain, anger and boredom. (p. 28)

■ In 2003, the RSPCA received 1,279,953 calls including requests for welfare advice, reports of injured or trapped animals, or reports of suspected neglect or suffering. (p. 30)

■ Fur, once the dirty word of fashion, is back with a vengeance and, apparently, without a guilty conscience. Mink and chinchilla are making a brazen reappearance on the catwalk and women who previously wouldn't be seen dead wearing a dead animal are draping themselves in pelts. (p. 32)

■ While Britain's attitude to fur remains largely dominated by conscience – though thanks to the celebrities recently seen draped in furs, that may be changing – the markets in Europe, the US and Russia are booming. (p. 33)

■ Every year, over 50 million animals are killed so that their fur can be used by the fashion industry; that's more than 130,000 animals slaughtered every day just so that someone else can wear their coats. (p. 34)

■ In Scotland, fur farming was banned in 2002, and in England and Wales in 2003. However, furs from animals farmed abroad can still be sold in the UK. (p. 35)

■ Farmed furs (mink and fox) are the mainstay of the fur trade, accounting for approximately 85 per cent of the industry's turnover. (p. 37)

■ Fur farming provides a livelihood for many thousands of individuals in Europe and North America. In Europe, there are some 6,000 fur farms, providing full-time employment to 30,000 individuals. (p. 39)

You might like to contact the following organisations for further information. Due to the increasing cost of postage, many organisations cannot respond to enquiries unless they receive a stamped, addressed envelope.

Advocates for Animals
10 Queensferry Street
Edinburgh, EH2 4PG
Tel: 0131 225 6039
Fax: 0131 220 6377
E-mail:
enquiries@advocatesforanimals.org.uk
Website:
www.advocatesforanimals.org.uk
One of the UK's leading animal
protection organisations.

Animal Aid
The Old Chapel
Bradford Street
Tonbridge
Kent, TN9 1AW
Tel: 01732 364546
Fax: 01732 366533
E-mail: info@animalaid.org.uk
Website: www.animalaid.org.uk
Aims to expose and campaign
peacefully against the abuse of
animals in all its forms and to
promote a cruelty-free lifestyle.

The Association of the British Pharmaceutical Industry (ABPI)
12 Whitehall
London
SW1A 2DY
Tel: 020 7930 3477
Fax: 020 7747 1414
Website: www.abpi.org.uk
ABPI is the trade association for
about a hundred companies in the
UK producing prescription
medicines.

The British Union for the Abolition of Vivisection (BUAV)
16a Crane Grove
London
N7 8NN
Tel: 020 7700 4888
Fax: 020 7700 0252
E-mail: info@buav.org
Website: www.buav.org
The BUAV opposes animal
experiments. They believe animals
are entitled to respect and
compassion which animal
experiments deny them.

Christian Medical Fellowship (CMF)
Partnership House
157 Waterloo Road
London, SE1 8XN
Tel: 020 7928 4694
Fax: 020 7620 2453
E-mail: admin@cmf.org.uk
Website: www.cmf.org.uk
Founded in 1949 and has over
4,500 British doctor members in all
branches of medicine, and over
1,000 student members.

Coalition for Medical Progress
Hamilton House
Mabledon Place
London, WC1H 9BB
Tel: 020 7953 0270
Fax: 020 7953 0271
Website: www.medicalprogress.org
The role of CMP is to help explain
the case for medical progress and
the benefits brought about by
animal research.

Countryside Alliance
The Old Town Hall
367 Kennington Road
London, SE11 4PT
Tel: 020 7840 9200
Fax: 020 7793 8484
E-mail: info@countryside-
alliance.org
Website: www.countryside-
alliance.org
Campaigns for rural livelihood.
They have 95,000 full members
and reflect the views of a further
350,000 affiliated members.

Dr Hadwen Trust
84a Tilehouse Street
Hitchin, SG5 2DY
Tel: 01462 436819
Fax: 01462 436844
E-mail: info@drhadwentrust.org.uk
Website:
www.drhadwentrust.org.uk
Promotes the development of
humane non-vivisectionist
techniques of research without the
use of living animals in order to
replace animals experiments in
science and medicine.

Huntingdon Life Sciences
Woolley Road
Alconbury
Huntingdon
Cambridgeshire, PE28 4HS
Tel: 01480 892000
Fax: 01480 590693
Website: www.huntingdon.com
Huntingdon Life Sciences is one of
the world's foremost product
development companies.

International Fur Trade Federation (IFTF)
PO Box 495
Weybridge
Surrey
KY13 8WD
E-mail: info@iftf.com
Website: www.iftf.com
The IFTF is an independent
international federation of
national fur trade associations and
organisations.

League Against Cruel Sports
Sparling House
83/87 Union Street
London, SE1 1SG
Tel: 020 7403 6155
Fax: 020 7403 4532
Website: www.league.uk.com
The League Against Cruel Sports
maintains a unique approach to
the protection of wildlife –
combining campaigning with
conservation. The League has been
at the forefront of the campaign to
ban hunting with dogs.

Royal Society for the Prevention of Cruelty to Animals (RSPCA)
Wilberforce Way
Southwater
Horsham
West Sussex
RH13 9RS
Tel: 0870 33 55 999
Fax: 0870 75 30 284
Website: www.rspca.org.uk
The RSPCA is a charity and the
world's oldest animal welfare
organisation.

INDEX

Agarose Diffusion Method 18
AIDS, and medical research 12, 13
anaesthesia, and animal experiments 6, 8, 9, 12, 22
angling 26
Animal Aid
    on animal rights 28-9
    on the Hunting Act 23-4
Animal Century 24
animal cruelty 28-9
    and abuse 28
    and animal welfare law 29-30
        reasons for 31
    education in preventing 31
    and the fur trade 32-3
    and RSPCA inspectors 30
    statistics 30-1
animal experiments 1-19
    alternatives to 7, 9, 10, 13-14, 17
        clinical studies 7, 18
        computer research 13-14, 17
        encouraging the use of 17
        epidemiology (population studies) 17
        questions and answers on 17
        reasons for not using 17
        reasons for using 17
        tissue and cell cultures 14, 17
    and animal rights activists 2, 9
    arguments against 2, 5-7
    arguments for 2, 9
    benefits of in scientific research 3
    on cats and dogs 1, 5, 8, 18,
    and fears of endangering patients 19
    and genetic research 11
    and genetically modified animals 1, 8
    and the law 16
    and meat-eaters 11
    and medical advances 10-11
    and moral justification 7
    on primates 1, 4, 8, 16, 18
    questions and answers on 10-11
    regulation of 1-2, 16, 18, 19
    replacement of 9
    research areas 1
    statistics 1, 4, 8
    and the three Rs 2
    and toxicological procedures 8, 10
    types of animals used in 1, 5-6, 8
        and the law 18
    types of premises used 6
    unreliability of 6
    and veterinary research 10
    see also medicines
animal rights 28-9
animal rights activists
    and animal experiments 2, 9, 11

laws against 15-16
    media coverage of 11
antibiotics, and medical research 12
asthma, and medical research 13

badger digging 24
Bonner, Tim 27
British Deer Society (BDS) 25
British Field Sports Society 23
British Union for the Abolition of Vivisection (BUAV)
    4, 5-7, 19
Brown, Nathan 26
Burns Report on hunting 20, 21, 22

Cambridge University, and animal research 16
Campbell, Naomi 32-3
cancer research, and animal experiments 8, 10, 13
Cass, Brian 15
cats, in animal experiments 1, 5, 8, 20,
cell culture 14, 17
childhood leukaemia, and medical research 12
China, animal research in 9
Clarke, Charles 21
clinical studies, as a research technique 7
Coalition for Medical Progress 18
Code for Crown Prosecutors, and animal cruelty
    cases 31
computer research, in medicine 13-14, 17
Countryside Alliance 20-1, 23, 27
Crawford, Cindy 32, 33

deer hunting 20, 24
    with helicopters 25
diseases, and medical research 12-13, 16
doctors, and animal experiments 19
dogs
    in animal experiments 1, 5, 8, 9, 18
    ban of docking of tails 29
Dr Hadwen Trust 17-18, 19
drag hunting 20-1, 22
drug development, and animal experiments 2-3, 9, 10,
    11, 13

epidemiology (population studies) 17
European Union (EU), and fur farming 35

farmers, and hunting 23
fashion, and the fur trade 32-3
fishing 26
foot-and-mouth disease, and the ban on hunting 22
fur trade 36-9
    and captive animals 34
    and supermodels 32-3
    trapping methods 35
    and wild animals 34-5

fur farming 38-39
  and animal welfare 39
  and farming methods 39

gender therapy 11
genetically modified animals, experiments on 1, 8
genetics research 11, 13
Glivec 9
Gold, Mark 24
goldfish, and animal welfare law 29
government departments, and animal experiments 6
Greet, Tim 29

hare coursing 21, 22, 23
Hawkins, Penny 4
heart disease, and medical research 12
helicopters, deer hunting with 25
hepatitis C 13
human rights, and animal rights 29
hunting 20-27
  arguments against 22
  arguments for 20-1
  badger digging 24
  before the ban 22
  Burns Report on 20, 21, 22
  clothes worn 21
  and the control of wild animals 21
  and the Countryside Alliance 20-1, 23, 27
  and cruelty 21, 22
  deer hunting 20, 24
    with helicopters 25
  drag hunting 20-1, 22
  fox numbers and the ban on 22
  hare coursing 21, 22, 23
  history of the abolition of 23-4
  and hounds 20
  hunt saboteurs 24, 26
  killing the fox 20
  law on (Hunting Act 2004) 22, 23
    testing enforcement of 27
  otter hunting 24
  public attitudes to 20, 21
  questions and answers on 20-1
  Scott Henderson Report on 23-4
Huntingdon Life Sciences 3, 9, 15
Huskisson, Mike 24

immunisation, and animal diseases 12
in vitro (in glass) research 14, 17
International Fur Trade Federation (IFTF) 36-9

Jagger, Elizabeth 30

Kennel Club 29

League Against Cruel Sports 22, 23, 24, 27
leukaemia, and medical research 12
Lopez, Jennifer 33
Lyons, Dan 4

Macdonald, Julien 32

meat-eaters, and opposition to animal experiments 11
media, portrayal of animal rights activists 11
medical advances, and animal experiments 10-11
medicines
  animal testing of 1, 11, 12-14
    drug development 2-3, 9, 10, 11, 13
    harmonising regulations 14
mental illness, and medical research 12
mice, in animal experiments 1, 4, 8
minks, and the fur trade 33, 34

National Trust, and deer hunting 25
Nicolson, Mark 25

otter hunting 24

pets
  and animal experiments 5
  and animal welfare law 29
pharmaceutical companies, and animal experiments 9,
    12-14
police, and the law on hunting 27
population studies (epidemiology) 17
pregnancy testing 17
pregnant animals, experiments on 18
primates, in animal experiments 1, 4, 8, 16, 18

Quorn Hunt 23, 24

Raven, Andrew 25
Remicade 9
RSPCA
  on animal experiments 4
  and animal welfare law 30-1
  and hunting 23, 24

scientific research, and animal experiments 3
Scotland, deer hunting in 25
supermodels, and the wearing of fur 32-3
surgery, and animal research 3

Thalidomide, and animal research 18
Thomas, Aubrey 26
tissue cultures 17
Tomlinson, Heather 9

universities
  and animal experiments 6, 16
  and animal rights activitists 15

veterinary research 10
Vlasak, Jerry 1

Walker, Alice 29
weapons testing, animal experiments in 1
Wetton, Dave 26
wild animals
  in animal experiments 6
  and the fur trade 34-5
  and fur farming 38-9
  see also hunting

ACKNOWLEDGEMENTS

The publisher is grateful for permission to reproduce the following material.

While every care has been taken to trace and acknowledge copyright, the publisher tenders its apology for any accidental infringement or where copyright has proved untraceable. The publisher would be pleased to come to a suitable arrangement in any such case with the rightful owner.

Chapter One: Animal Experiments

Animal experimentation, © 2004 Christian Medical Fellowship, *The benefits of animals in scientific research*, © Huntingdon Life Sciences, *Animals experiments at 10-year high*, © Telegraph Group Limited, London 2005, *Introduction to animal experiments*, © BUAV, *Species used in experiments in 2003*, © BUAV, *Scientific procedures on live animals 2003*, © Crown copyright is reproduced with the permission of Her Majesty's Stationery Office, *Procedures*, © Crown copyright is reproduced with the permission of Her Majesty's Stationery Office, *If mice could talk*, © Guardian Newspapers Limited 2005, *Animal experiments*, © Animal Aid, *Animals in medicines*, © ABPI – The Association of the British Pharmaceutical Industry, *Who will stand up for animal experiments?*, © spiked 2000-2005, *Alternatives*, © Dr Hadwen Trust, *The law*, © Coalition for Medical Progress 2005, *Concern*, © MORI, *Distrust among doctors*, © Ooze Online 2005.

Chapter Two: The Hunting Debate

Hunting FAQs, © Countryside Alliance, *96% say enforcing hunt ban should not be Clarke's priority*, © Countryside Alliance, *Hunting with dogs*, © League Against Cruel Sports, *A great day for wildlife*, © Animal Aid, *Charity angered by deer hunting with helicopters*, © Telegraph Group Limited, London 2005, *New era dawns for the 'antis'*, © Telegraph Group Limited, London 2005, *Hunts intend to push new law to the limit*, © Telegraph Group Limited, London 2005.

Chapter Three: Animal Welfare

Animal rights, © Animal Aid, *Animal cruelty law*, © Telegraph Group Limited, London 2005, *Do your duty*, © RSPCA, *Comparison with other bodies taking prosecutions*, © RSPCA, *Fashion's new F-word*, © Associated Newspapers Ltd, *The facts about the fur trade*, © Advocates for Animals, *International fur trade today*, © International Fur Trade Federation, *Fur farming*, © International Fur Trade Federation.

Photographs and illustrations:

Pages 1, 24: Pumpkin House; pages 4, 12, 20, 27, 32, 36: Simon Kneebone; pages 6, 19, 35: Angelo Madrid; pages 11, 16, 23, 35: Don Hatcher; pages 14, 28: Bev Aisbett.

Craig Donnellan
Cambridge
April, 2005